OVERPAID, OVER-SEXED AND OVER THERE

CHRIS HOLLOWAY spent ten years as a resident in the United States where, apart from two years' reluctant service in the armed forces, he worked at Cunard Line's North American head office in New York. Transferred back to the company's UK head office in 1966, he later worked in other sectors of travel before leaving the industry to teach tourism. Chris retired as Professor of Tourism Management at the University of the West of England in 1997. He is the author of two bestselling textbooks on the tourism industry, *The Business of Tourism* and *Marketing for Tourism*, both published by Pearson.

Published in paperback by SilverWood Books 2009

www.silverwoodbooks.co.uk

ISBN 978-1-906236-16-8

British Library Cataloguing in Publication Data

A CIP catalogue record for this book is available from the British Library

Set in Adobe Garamond Pro by SilverWood Books

Printed on FSC paper in the United Kingdom by Cpod, Trowbridge, Wiltshire

Mixed Sources
Product group from well-managed
forests and other controlled sources
www.fsc.org Cert no. TT-COC-2082
© 1996 Forest Stewardship Council

FSC

OVERPAID, OVER-SEXED, AND OVER THERE.

CHRIS HOLLOWAY

SilverWood

CONTENTS

PLATES AND IMAGES

PLATES AND IMAGES CONT'D

OVERPAID, OVER-SEXED AND OVER THERE

PROLOGUE

Anyone familiar with the classic film and TV series M*A*S*H will be aware of the rich vein of humour which runs through life in military service. Where that service was involuntary – as it was for millions of young men obliged to undergo eighteen months to two years of military service (known as National Service in the UK, or the Draft in the USA) between the 1940s and 60s – somehow the humour is heightened by the contrast between what we like to think of as normal everyday civilian life and the almost surrealistic experience of day to day life in the armed forces.

Spike Milligan exploited these contrasts to the full and was one of a number of humorous writers who have entertained us with stories about their life in uniform; yet curiously (and *pace* the Foreign Legion) few seem to have ventured to record their experiences as conscripts in the armies of other nations – least of all that of the USA. This is all the more surprising given the millions of immigrants who, between the end of World War II and the 1960s, dutifully fulfilled their military obligations in the armed services of the United States, en route to citizenship.

Since returning to the UK more than forty years ago, I have regaled countless friends and acquaintances with anecdotes from my life in the US Army, a period which I look back on with great affection, and some bemusement at how this enormous institution was able to function at all, let alone with sometimes surprising efficiency. At the time, the US Army comprised upwards of two million men, a rag-bag assortment of often ill-educated, and sometimes illiterate, regulars from the fifty states interspersed with immigrants from the four corners of the world, quite a number of whom lacked even basic knowledge of the English language. These were interspersed with young inductees, often including highly-educated professionals from Ivy League universities. From this clash of cultures emerged the anecdotes which I have enjoyed recounting, and which I felt deserved a wider audience.

Over time, I began to jot these stories down, gradually drawing them into a sequence of events reflecting the not untypical life of a conscript of the time. As time went on, I began to realise that what I was recording was not merely the humour of life in the army, but a social history of the time which could be enjoyed equally by the many inductees on both sides of the pond, and by anyone with an interest in life during the 1950s and 60s.

For readers who are inclined to disbelieve some or all of what they read here, I can promise that every word and event is true, with very little embellishment. For those cast in a less than salutary light, names have been changed to protect their reputations, but where it has been necessary to retain real names (such as those of the famous American football star Rosie Grier) then those names will appear, but it goes without saying always in a positive light. Where the names are authentic, they appear exactly as given. Gwenneth Fillingame and Squeaky Putnam are very real people. So was Elvis Presley.

I hope you enjoy reading this as much as I enjoyed writing it, and that for many older readers it will bring back some affectionate memories.

Chris Holloway
Bristol 2009

This book is dedicated to
the countless befuddled and disenfranchised immigrants
who so loyally served in the armed forces of the
United States, their adopted country, in the middle years
of the twentieth century, and who hopefully gained as
much as I did from the experience

CHAPTER 1

In which the Limey learns to love New York,
and finds he is to be drafted

On a glorious sunny morning in May, 1956, RMS *Queen Mary* nudged her way up the Hudson River, squeezing between the boroughs of Staten Island and Brooklyn as she sought out her home dock at Pier 90, on Manhattan's west side. To the lay observer, the vessel suddenly took on an appearance of serious instability, disgorging her passengers from below decks to cram shoulder to shoulder on the uppermost deck; wide-eyed tourists from Europe, nervous immigrants from all four corners of the globe and damp-eyed homecoming Americans, all keen to catch their first glimpse of the 'old lady' – the Statue of Liberty – off the port bow.

She didn't let us down. Caught in the warm sunlight against a clear blue sky, her dazzling green patina shone like the gloriously clichéd beacon of hope she had become, pristine, elegant...

At least that was the initial impression, soon put right when I borrowed a neighbour's binoculars and got a disheartening close-up of the old lady. Her crown, arm and lamp pitted with rust, she looked more of a mind to encourage potential settlers to turn round and catch the first ship back. Was this perhaps some cunning plan hatched by the authorities to reduce immigration? "Give me your tired, your poor, your huddled masses – and I'll pop them on the next eastbound crossing."

The view beyond her was still less gratifying, a tumble of broken down warehouses, shacks and ugly high rises which in my ignorance I first took to be the Manhattan skyline, until I realised I was looking west and what I was staring at with such horror was in fact the heavily industrial New Jersey riverbank – at that time, in an advanced state of decay.

Moving to the starboard side of the ship proved to be more rewarding; the great skyline of Manhattan's high-rise buildings, familiar to us all through photos and films, glittered a welcome to the tired, the poor and the merely avaricious – those economic migrants, like me, keen for a share of the gravy train which we all understood America to represent in the booming mid-50s.

Once past the statue the journey became all too short and it seemed only a matter of minutes before the Moran tugs, which had joined us a few miles out at sea, began to nose us into place at the pier. This is no easy task – sideways on, the great ship virtually filled the entire gap between the City and the opposing New Jersey shoreline. The final process of docking took some time, and gave me the chance to observe just how challenging it is to move a vessel of this size in strictly limited space.

At that point, I could not have guessed in my wildest dreams that within a few weeks I would myself – as an employee of Cunard – be helping to tie up this behemoth when the New York longshoremen took the decision to strike for more money. This situation arose with monotonous but most welcome regularity (office staff sent down to the pier earned anything up to five times their regular salary, in tips from embarking passengers). I still remember clearly when, on one of those occasions, with tugboat crews out in sympathy, the *Queen Mary*'s Master ignored advice from the pilots and decided to dock her without assistance. For all his mastery of seamanship, he succeeded in taking six feet off the end of the pier in the process.

From the moment of disembarkation the world changed for me. In a state of utter confusion, and surrounded by mountains of baggage – of which my two cases looked quite the sorriest – I, all of 22 years of age, felt totally lost. Although immigration and customs formalities had been completed on board before arrival, I had little knowledge of the city, no plans on where I would be staying, and in the mêlée I wasn't even sure how to get off the pier.

The decision was soon out of my hands. An enormous longshoreman, fully six feet in height and almost as broad, bore down on me and with a barely intelligible Bronx accent demanded, with a glance towards my two pathetic bags, "Are these yours?"

It's difficult to convey the scorn which accompanied these three words, but they carried a clear message – that he, a man more accustomed to the world of Louis Vuitton, would be transporting my battered cases under duress. Picking them up without waiting for a reply, he vanished in the direction of the street. Fearing I was about to lose my few worldly possessions, I had little choice but to follow.

At the foot of the steps leading down to the street, and still fifty feet from the nearest cab rank, he deposited both cases and held out an enormous hand. I thrust a handful of coins into them, which he regarded for a moment with distain followed by a closer scrutiny clearly intended to identify and remove the anticipated buttons or foreign coins.

Suitably mortified, I stooped to collect my cases – only to find them whisked out of my hand by yet another longshoreman, even broader of frame, who proceeded to carry them a further ten paces from the steps to the taxi rank, whereupon another open hand appeared under my face.

I began to see that America was going to come expensive.

Anyone who believes that American English bears a close resemblance to the language we speak on this side of the pond will be in for a shock when they land in New York. My first experience of the gap separating the two languages occurred even before stepping into the taxi. Glancing at a nearby news stand, the front page headline of the *New York Daily News* caught my eye: 'See Goons in Reisel Blinding'.

Intrigued, I had to buy the paper and, after a lengthy tussle, was given to understand that a certain Victor Reisel, an investigative journalist, had been subjected to an acid attack which the press was blaming on criminal elements in the city. Once you get the hang of this form of short-hand, everything falls into place. The classic news headline, which reveals just how effective US journalistic brevity can be, was 'Sox ink Flowers', by which three worded code the news was conveyed to the great American public that the Boston Red Sox baseball team had signed on a player by the surname of Flowers.

But newspeak isn't the only obstacle facing a speaker of the Queen's English on arrival in America. One of my first tasks was to learn how to order breakfast in a café. You need to know whether you want your eggs 'easy over' or 'sunny side up' to start with, while an order for a toasted English shouldn't automatically lead one to assume cannibalism is rife. Hash browns, hominy grits, blackeye peas, sausages bathed in maple syrup, bacon slices so rigid and overcooked they fell to pieces when pierced with a fork – a whole host of gastronomic delights which constitute the American breakfast was opening up for me.

However, when the complications of American language are

compounded by the use of army abbreviation and terminology, comprehension becomes tougher. Just six months after landing, I was struggling with a missive that had reached me via the US mail:

Subject: Orders   29 Jan 57
To: Inductee Concerned
PAC UMT & SVC Act 1951, as amended, fol pers have been inducted this date in the AUS at USA RMS, NY, 39 Whitehall Street, NY4, NY, In grade Pvt (E-1) SSN 006, for a period of Twenty-four (24) months, unless sooner discharged by proper auth, are asgd to US Army Reception Station, Ft. Dix, Ft. Dix, NJ for proc and subs asgmt. WP 29 Jan 57 ETA 2400 hrs 29 Jan 57 ETS 28 Jan 59 PCS TDN 2172010 701-4 P1311-02 S99-999. Tvl by bus, rail, and/or mil and coml aircraft is auth. Tvl by privately owned conveyance not authorised. In accordance with AR 55-65 and par 5052 JTR, TO will furn nec meal tickets as required. AUTH: DA Msg 482654, AGPA-NA, dated 19 Dec 56.

An initial reading left me with the feeling that it might as well have been written in Serbo-Croat, but I applied myself and eventually the gist became clear.

I was about to become a committed, if reluctant, member of the glorious army of these United States; to be transported, together with a group of ill-assorted and equally unwilling burghers from New York suburbia, away from my life of relative ease, working in a comfortable, air-conditioned downtown New York office, to take up abode in a grim and undoubtedly

21

freezing (this was, after all, January, and temperatures hovered around the −30 mark) barracks in the wilds of New Jersey – a State which up to that point (apart from that shock preview from the *Queen Mary*) I had experienced only through its delightful sandy beaches at the height of summer.

And here I was, just two weeks later, duly reporting to USA RMS (whatever that was) in downtown Manhattan, preparing for my life as a reluctant GI. My companions on the journey into the future were to include fellow New Yorkers with such exotic names as Barbagallo, Egizi, Matisons, Pervelis, Pretzell, Rodriguez-Fratiselli and Slotnick – in other words, the usual gloriously cross-cultural collection of racial, ethnic and religious minorities to be found on every New York City street corner. Piled into our army transport, and in various states of psychological disorientation, we headed off to New Jersey convinced only in the belief that, at best, we were in for twenty-four months of blood, toil, tears and sweat, to be relieved only by occasional opportunities for rape and pillage in some foreign field.

The journey gave me time to ruminate. Just a few hours earlier I had stood alongside several dozen other hapless and bewildered young males, raising my right hand to take the oath of allegiance, promising to fight and defeat the enemies of the United States, whoever they might be, and suffering only the mildest trepidation at the thought that Britain and America might engage in yet another post-colonial conflagration that could severely exercise a challenge to my loyalties. Still a British subject, I wondered at the ability of a country to which I owed no allegiance – where I was denied the right to vote, yet regularly contributed taxes on my earnings (isn't that what the Boston Tea Party was all about? 'No taxation without representation' came to mind) – to draft me for two whole years into what was for me a foreign army, while at the same time expecting me, if called upon, to fight anyone, including my own country.

I wondered whether I should raise this as a philosophical issue with the recruiting sergeant who was administering our oath, but one glance told me this wasn't the ideal time, and he didn't look like the kind of man who made a practice of philosophical discussion. So I meekly kept my hand in the air.

Of course, I could have gone home. What was my legal position? Surely going AWOL even before induction and disappearing back to my home country wasn't an extraditable offence? But after sleeping on it, common sense had taken over. I was, after all, in the country of my own free will, having fought for two years to obtain an immigrant visa. I had already spent six months working in New York City, loving every moment of it. There was no war on (this being the all too brief lull between Korea and Vietnam) so I felt confident that there was a reasonable chance of my emerging alive and in one piece at the end of the two years. But above all I felt a reluctance to give up my life in my chosen country, having worked so hard to get here in the first place.

I was nevertheless puzzled at how I had landed myself in this predicament. I had felt reasonably confident that my rejection from call-up for the British Army on medical grounds would be enough to ensure the continuation of life on easy street. When my assessment came through the post (Classification 1A: fully acceptable for induction into the US Armed Forces) requiring me to report for induction a fortnight later, I was horrified. I fruitlessly waved my exemption from the British Army at the induction centre – until in dawned on me that the US Army takes anyone, as long as they're capable of standing up and they're not a close friend of a senator, State governor or Hollywood film producer, to provide cannon fodder for their innumerable escapades abroad. I could hardly blame them – I had, after all, passed a medical in order to get my US visa in the first place. However, had this all occurred just a decade later, with the Vietnam War claiming casualties on a daily basis, I would undoubtedly have been on the first plane home.

So it was that I accepted inevitability, and the assignment of a number – US51396820 – which would identify me as a GI for the next twenty-four months.

Funny, isn't it, how one remembers an army number? I frequently go into a blind panic trying to remember my simple four number passwords for credit and debit cards, and on occasion have even been known to forget my own phone number when trying to call home... but my army number is seared into my mind forever.

The day was already well advanced when our bus arrived at Fort Dix, some 100 miles southwest of New York City and then, as now, a leading training ground for new army recruits in the north-eastern States. We were greeted by a less-than-effusive sergeant who did his best to line us up into some semblance of military order and then marched us into the reception centre.

I looked around at my fellow recruits and was put in mind of that wonderful comedy film *Carry on, Sergeant* in which a rag-bag assortment of recruits is built into an efficient fighting force with just a few weeks of basic training. I tried to envisage a similar transformation being carried out on this motley crew, who at that point bore a passing resemblance to the tattered soldiers portrayed in the famous painting of Washington crossing the Delaware.

In the reception area we were welcomed (I use the term loosely) by an officer who gave the impression of being both tired of life and resentful at the way the army had assigned him to his present role. He addressed us tersely and without warmth, warning us against our considering suicide under any circumstances, because the paperwork he would then face was interminable and would take up far too much of his valuable time. He spoke as if this particular form of paperwork had come to feature as a large element in his daily tasks, and clearly expected our sympathy with this imposition. There followed details as to what we could expect if he found anyone ignoring the warning.

Looking around at my fellow inductees, some of whom were by this point clearly suffering stress, I realised that many had never been away from home before, and a few looked as though they might well have been considering extreme measures.

The officer's address appeared to have some effect, although quite why any punishment the army could think to impose would be perceived as having a potentially more catastrophic result than that of their own suicide – and how such punishment were to be carried out should they choose to ignore the order – were not issues that the sad sacks being addressed spent much time considering.

We learned that our basic training was to extend over eight weeks, followed by a further eight weeks of advanced training during which we would be expected to acquire the necessary skills to fit us into a suitable slot during the remaining twenty months of our service. No leave would be granted until the satisfactory completion of the first eight weeks. I was assigned to Co P, Second Training Regiment, and promptly marched off with a number of colleagues to the barracks that were to be our home for the next two months.

Our first day was memorable, and marked by that common army expression 'hurry up and wait'. The sheer number of lines (queues to those of you on this side of the pond) in which we were obliged to wait interminably during those first hours, drawing kit, being assigned a lethal weapon and being fed (half an hour to eat, and if you were last in line you had ten minutes to wolf it down; my stomach never fully recovered from this maltreatment) made the day simultaneously mind-blowingly dull and totally exhausting.

Drawing our own weapon was an experience generating mixed feelings. The possession of a weapon – an M1 rifle – capable of blowing someone's brains out gives one a sense of both power and terror (although we failed to realise at the time that the issue of live ammunition would normally be restricted to our brief appearances on the firing range). NCOs charged with the responsibility to issue rifles are evidently trained to provide an identical line of patter: first, to admonish us never to refer to this as a 'gun', because this term was to be restricted to heavier calibre weapons such as a field artillery piece. We were then advised that, for the next twenty-four months, our rifle was to act as a replacement for our wives or girlfriends, and we were to treat it as if it were every bit as precious. We were to guard it with our lives, to keep it clean, to never let it out of our sight. This, of course, offered numerous opportunities for *double entendres* about similarities in possible relationships and comparisons between girlfriends and personal weapons, which led to some good-natured banter and helped to loosen up some of the more stressed among us.

Drawing army issue clothing is an interesting exercise for anyone who has had experience of army clothing in Europe, where uniforms are (or certainly were at that time) generally ill-fitting and of poor quality. By contrast, the US Army went to considerable effort to ensure that their uniforms, especially boots, fitted well; where necessary, even tailor-made alterations could be made to improve the fit. Still more impressive was the sheer quality of the materials used, and the fact that we were issued with both a full summer and winter set of uniforms, including distinctive dress hats and duty hats for both winter and summer. I can recall that, on a first visit back to Britain in full winter uniform some months later, I was actually saluted in the street by an English private, clearly overwhelmed by my combination of well pressed dress uniform, dress hat and array of medallions on my chest (mainly awards for marksmanship in basic training, but each bearing a passing resemblance to the Victoria Cross).

As in the British Army, enormous attention was given to polishing equipment, although there seemed to be rather less brass involved in US equipment, a welcome relief. Boots, however, were the usual focus of attention, and we were obliged to ensure that these were sufficiently highly polished to allow the inspecting officers to see their faces in the toe. I am eternally in the debt of one young New Yorker who had made the discovery that a popular brand of underarm deodorant stick known as Mennen 'Brake' produced a shine of almost unbelievable intensity, when applied to leather, thus saving us all endless trouble. What this did to the leather, we didn't concern ourselves with, as long as the boots got us through basic training. I have often wondered if the manufacturers of this product ever became aware of its devious use in the army, or whether their marketing staff wondered why members of the US forces needed such high levels of underarm protection.

When we finally turned in for the night, I discovered that our bedding in the barracks actually included sheets and pillowcases. I was overwhelmed, contrasting this cornucopia with what I had observed being issued to British National Servicemen, on visits to army barracks back home. Issue of clothing and equipment was not completed until well after midnight, by which time we were all ready to collapse.

It seemed that scarcely had we fallen into bed and closed

our eyes after 'lights out' than we found ourselves being shaken awake and bawled at by a sergeant to "Moooove your asses .... NOW!"

I looked at my watch. It was 3.30 a.m. Feeling that some dreadful mistake had been made, I rolled over to get back to sleep again, a practice that failed to engender the NCO's sympathy. Scarcely aware of what I was doing, I stumbled with some 60 other sleepwalkers towards the ablutions – but given just ten minutes to dress and report for morning assembly, these were sketchy at best.

On Day Two, one of our first obligations was a haircut. This surprised me, as I had taken care to get a short but, I thought, suitably stylish, haircut just a couple of days earlier, to avoid facing the demon barbers of the military. When I pointed this out to the NCO in charge, he seemed to find it amusing. Without deigning to reply, he merely pointed to the line. Others who had taken a more extreme line with their hair styles, some much shorter than mine, were similarly ushered into line, and we realised that the haircut wasn't an option. All of us would be subjected to this indignity, even those who had hair so short it was all but invisible. It was evident that professional barber training in the US military was cursory. It entailed not so much haircutting as shaving, leaving us to all intents and purposes bald. Bearing in mind that this was mid-winter, this wasn't a welcome start to military life.

Thereafter, we faced a barrage of tests, including two tests of intelligence. The first was a test of spatial ability at which I have always been totally incompetent. This time was no exception – I managed to record an IQ of 74, thus placing me at near-Neanderthal level. On the second test I somehow managed to achieve a score of 134. Following these two tests, I was told that I was officer material (whether based on the first or second test,

I was not enlightened) but any thoughts in this direction were quashed when I pointed out that I was not yet a citizen (and anyway, this would have required me to serve a minimum of three rather than two years, which was a sufficiently strong barrier to reject the idea from the outset, as far as I was concerned).

The barracks at Fort Dix resemble nothing so much as a vast colonial-style pre-1950s holiday camp; row upon row of clapboard white-painted two-storey buildings, all identical in design and size, so that a new inductee could spend his opening days searching for hours on end to find his own base. Inside each, serried ranks of double bunks, beds encased tightly enough in their ubiquitous khaki blankets to guarantee the bouncing of a coin when dropped by our humourless barracks sergeant on his morning rounds. A tall, narrow metal wardrobe, painted a dark green, for uniforms. A footlocker, also dark green, for other army issue (at this stage in army life almost all civilian possessions are forbidden) completed the furniture.

The appearance of each room was made still starker by their gleaming wooden floors, polished and honed through years of exhaustive cleaning as a prelude to inspections; minimalist modernists would love it. Decoration was limited to a poster on the central pillars. This showed a picture of George Washington in military garb, proclaiming his disdain for soldiers who used foul language, and admonishing us to refrain. I never found that this had the slightest impact, either on the inductees or the regular cadre, all of whom swore like the troopers they were. The level of day-to-day language can be best appreciated when it is revealed that the common term for the headgear worn in duty uniform was a 'cunt cap' – a vivid, and, I must admit, effectively descriptive term for this piece of uniform. The term was in such frequent use that it had become semi-official, with sergeants cheerfully bawling at morning assemblies, "All troops will wear ties and cunt caps on parade tomorrow". Remember, this was in the late 1950s, when such words *never* appeared in print, let alone on the screen. Its initial incongruity and its impact on us was lost on the NCOs who addressed us, and it wasn't long before the term had become a familiar part of our own language.

I was assigned to an upper bunk in my barracks (or more truthfully, was beaten in the rush to secure lower beds) to which I retired at the earliest opportunity. Scarcely had I laid my head on my pillow, when I found myself propelled vertically towards the ceiling, the entire frame of the double bunk shuddering as the enormous bulk of my bunk-mate collapsed on the bed below. This was my introduction to Rosie Grier, African-American doyen of the New York Giants American Football team, 300 lbs in his size 12 socks. Much later, he was to achieve his true moment of fame when, as bodyguard to Bobby Kennedy, he seized Kennedy's assassin Sirhan Sirhan and prevented further rounds being fired by jamming his own finger between the assassin's trigger and trigger guard.

Rosie was as intrigued by me as I was by him. I think it was his first encounter with an Englishman, but he had evidently watched British films, and insisted on calling me 'the block', which I believe was his understanding of the English term 'bloke'. Massively strong, he was capable of raising me on one hand above his head – a feat in which he indulged frequently and with great pleasure, as much to enjoy my discomfort as to revel in his own strength. Rosie complained endlessly of a back problem, and disappeared quietly before the completion of his basic training, I believe to take up his sports career as a member of the US Army team.

Chapter 2

In which the Limey learns to acclimatise
to life in the US Army

Rosie's departure left no shortage of colourful characters in my barracks. We were a strange mix, combining university graduates from Princeton, Yale and Harvard (who, having completed their degree programmes, were now eligible for the draft) with lads from southern States like Kentucky and West Virginia, some of whom were enjoying footwear for the first time in their lives. The latter were also intrigued to find a foreigner amongst them. "So you're English?" as one Kentuckian asked me. "Well, speak some of your language!"

Others wanted to know whether in England we had the benefit of electricity and, in one case, asked whether the English were accustomed to sleeping in beds, or on bales of hay. I thought initially that they might be gently ribbing me, but all too soon it dawned that they genuinely didn't know. The most extreme of these Neanderthals, with an IQ so low I wondered at his ability to be drafted, was a lad from the US Virgin Islands, who made a practice of masturbating into his hat.

"Aw, my Gawd!" wailed his bunk-mate, "he's beating off again..." and we would all throw pillows and boots at him.

Our disgust had, I believe, less to do with the fact that he was using his hat as a receptacle, and more with our fascinated realisation that he would be wearing the same headgear the following morning.

I soon bonded with the only other 'alien' in the barracks, Hans, a young man from the Sudetenland (formerly a German possession and by then part of Soviet-controlled Czechoslovakia). Given his place of birth, it was to be expected that the authorities would pay some attention to his background and affiliation – this was, after all, a period in American history during which the fear of a Communist insurrection was paramount in society. Hans was quizzed closely during the induction process, and was astonished to be shown data that the authorities had apparently already obtained about his earlier life. In his view, many of these facts could have been obtained only through investigations carried out behind the Iron Curtain – if true, an extraordinarily expensive procedure to go through for a mere inductee.

Later, Hans was to serve with special forces near Fort Churchill, Manitoba, testing prototype boots designed for wear in extreme temperatures, sometimes as low as –30º. He stuck this out for some six months, but finally could stand it no longer and asked for reassignment on compassionate grounds – whereupon he found himself transferred to test the same boots in the Mojave Desert, where temperatures were hitting 120º. Somehow, he emerged from these experiences unscathed both mentally and physically.

Undoubtedly, the strangest story emerging from adjoining barracks was that of an individual from one of the southern states who didn't appear to fit in with his surroundings in any way. Middle-aged and a rank or two above the rest of us, but still apparently undergoing basic training, he said little but refused point-blank to follow accepted procedures when pulling guard duty. Rather than marching smartly up and down with rifle at the slope, prepared at appropriate moments to challenge strangers with the recognised code ("Halt, who goes there?") as accepted practice had it, he would instead proceed to shin up a nearby tree, where he camouflaged himself while awaiting the arrival of the officer of the guard.

In due course, this gentleman arrived and, finding no sign of anyone carrying out guard duty, stepped out of his jeep to investigate. From a point somewhere above his head a calm but firm voice calling out in its soft, southern drawl, "OK, buddy, hold it right there."

The duty officer, a major, went ballistic. "What the hell do you think you're doing in that tree? Get your ass down here this instant."

"Major," came the quiet response, "In Ko'rea, ah got me a general, and ah guess ah'm about to get me a major."

There was a brief silence, while the major pondered his next course of action. Discretion being the better part of valour, and fearing a confrontation which could have possibly ended in gunfire, he retreated to his jeep and moved on, but made enquiries upon his return to base. It transpired that the soldier in question had indeed served in Korea, where – so the story goes – among other decorations he had apparently been awarded the Congressional Medal of Honor, the nation's highest decoration. Rumour had it that he was subsequently involved in some fracas in which a US general officer had been wounded, and in consequence our hero had been quietly retired from the army. Finding it impossible to adjust to civilian life, he had applied to re-enlist, and was reluctantly allowed to return to the life he loved providing he first undertook to complete another period of basic training.

The training cadre were equally memorable for their characters. The sergeant whose responsibility it was to get us through these first eight weeks spoke entirely in clichés, of which the most common was, "It behoves each and every one of you ...."

This was a phrase he would somehow manage to slip into almost any sentence with which he addressed us. Favourite admonishments ranged from "Wipe that shit-eating grin off your face," to "Don't just stand there with your thumb up your ass."

These became so familiar we were soon able to chorus the final words. Smoking was then widespread and permitted when 'at ease', but the army cadre, mindful of the need for their landscapes to be neat and orderly at all times, reminded us constantly to field strip our butts, following which all detritus was to be picked up and removed to the nearest garbage bins.

"Ah want to see asses and elbows," our sergeant exhorted us, as we scrambled to collect our rubbish.

Low-rank NCOs in training cadres are commonly expected to act like bullies, and happily fulfilled these expectations, rejoicing in the authority of their single or double stripes. We certainly had our share of these, but one corporal was much loved and respected, for failing to treat us as lower than cattle. Corporal Acciavati's name is forever embedded in my memory as a result of an episode which I still remember with fondness, a half century after the event. As he stood in front of the assembled troops anxious to impose his authority on us, by common consent and without apparent consultation, we simultaneously broke into a rousing chorus,

> *When the moon hits your eye*
> *like a big pizza pie,*
> *Acciavati!*

In spite of his best efforts to keep a straight face, Acciavati broke up, and never failed to do so on subsequent occasions

34

when we repeated the song – something which we did frequently because it helped to relieve the tedium of morning assemblies.

One cadre officer, Lt Dassauer, was an Anglophobe and consequently had taken an instant dislike to me. At our first encounter, he challenged me to justify the employment by the British Army of colonial troops during the Second World War. I was nonplussed, and it was thirty minutes later before a suitable rejoinder occurred to me – that the US Army was even then drafting young men from their own 'colonies' in Puerto Rico and the US Virgin Islands – but by then it was far too late for the quip. Probably just as well, or I would have ended up on a charge of insubordination.

By the second day of our basic training I had become aware of the American obsession with cleanliness, in the form of showers. At least two, sometimes three or four, were taken every day, first thing in the morning, last thing at night and whenever completing any period of intense physical activity. The American military shower is a serious affair. Water emerges not so much in the form of a spray as a series of fine jets that zap you like needles, hurling you across the floor and forcing you to hang on to any fixed object to prevent being swept out of the shower room.

"Gee, I gotta take a shower," was among the most frequent expressions to be heard when off-duty, and even if there remained only ten minutes before the next assignment, off they would go to the shower room, whence they would emerge a few minutes later with a beatific, practically post-coital smile on their faces. Mind you, what else they may have been getting up to in the shower room is beyond my knowledge.

One early episode in these shower rooms remains with me. Among the troopers in my barracks was a well-built, very tall lad from the mid-West whose aquiline features marked him out as of Native American extraction. At the end of our first busy day, we all headed for the showers apart from this man – let's call him Joe – who was busy reading his mail, seated at the foot of his bed. Most of us had finished showering and were back by our beds when he picked up his towel and walked to the showers. A few minutes later, as we were chattering and laughing together, he re-emerged from the shower, naked apart from a towel hung casually over his shoulder. One by one, as we caught sight of him, our conversations died away and we remained transfixed, our eyes fastened disbelievingly upon his nether regions. Within seconds, the entire barracks had fallen silent. Joe nonchalantly strolled to his bunk, seemingly unaware of our interest. This guy was huge – obscenely, grotesquely, enviably enormous. His tackle appeared to reach somewhere south of his knees. In the face of such evidence of manhood, strong men quailed, male porn stars are humbled, women with vivid imaginations would pass out.

From that day on Joe expected, and received, our unqualified respect and admiration.

Most of my basic training skills and knowledge are now little more than a fleeting memory. However I'd like to think that, if pushed, I would still be capable of stripping a rifle without a second's hesitation, or fixing a bayonet and, without so much as a by-your-leave, thrusting it into a straw bale decorated inartistically and inadequately to resemble a Red Army trooper.

What remains vividly in my memory is the sheer discomfort of so much of the experience. This was, after all, rural New Jersey in mid-winter, where the snow lay two feet thick on the ground. Outdoor lectures on field manoeuvres were held for two hours at a time while we sat in the bleachers, our backsides turning to ice and our eyebrows rimmed with icicles, uncomprehending as the words were snatched away from our cadres' mouths by

Fig 1 Ready for my first guard duty, Fort Dix, March 1957.

the howling winds and whirling snow flurries. Daytime was bad enough, but night manoeuvres were infinitely worse, with sub-zero temperatures the norm.

I recall one occasion when I stood with one foot buried knee-deep in a snow drift, the other foot and both arms waving horizontally in front of me like some inane slow-motion ballet routine (we were supposed to be feeling for invisible tripwires). The only thing passing through my mind was the question, "What the hell am I doing in this country, in this army, and whatever brought me to America in the first place?"

With the spectre of similar idiots strung out to my left and right, waving their feet in the air like zombies, I could, however, sense an affiliation as an honorary member of the Neanderthal community. Far worse was pulling guard duty at the shooting range where, alone and feeling abandoned, I marched faithfully up and down for my allotted hours, never seeing an officer of the day (who was sensibly tucked up in bed with no intention of paying a visit to the extremities of New Jersey in the small hours), until I was relieved and thankfully returned to the bliss of a warm barracks room.

Some field training could be fun – and some could be actually dangerous. At one point in our training, we were informed that we were to face live ammunition, which made us apprehensive until we heard that this entailed nothing more than crawling on our stomachs through muddy trenches while machine gunners fired live rounds, interspersed with tracer bullets, above our heads. We were informed that as long as we kept our heads and bottoms down, we would come to no harm. This was fine, as long as you weren't the panicky type, and all in Co P were calm and collected. Not so a young second lieutenant who was undertaking officer training from another outfit on the same day. Halfway through the ordeal, he leapt to his feet and ran screaming from the field. Somehow the gunners were able to restrain their fire, and he came to no harm... but I imagine this rather limited his opportunities to proceed towards an eventual commission.

A less attractive experience was the obligatory exposure to nerve gas. The theory training was fine – listen for the shout of "Gas!", whip out your gas mask while holding your breath, and put it on. We managed to master this after a few tries, and felt confident in our ability to respond quickly in the event that any enemy would employ such dastardly weapons. Then word filtered out that we were going to have to do this for real. The sergeant whose responsibility it was to take charge of this operation was a sadist, and his obvious enjoyment when he announced that gas practice would be taking place *that day* did nothing to dispel our concerns. Ordered to put on our masks, we were then lead into a Nissen hut, whereupon the nerve gas was released. After a few seconds, the order came to remove our masks and run like hell for the exits. We had some trouble with the first instruction, but none with the second, sprinting towards the end of the hut as if our lives depended on it. (Now I come to think of it, they probably did.) However, the fiendish cadre had devised the programme to ensure that, due to the length of the building, few could hold their breath long enough to actually avoid getting a quick whiff of the stuff, so we focussed on taking the shortest possible breath. The intention was clear – we needed to be able to recognise the smell when subject to attack in the field.

The only trouble was that all of us were in such a blind panic that the last thing on our minds was to think about what the wretched stuff smelled like. We were also instructed in the use of atropine injections to nullify its effects, but having seen several inductees collapse when inoculations were administered in the first days of basic training, I wasn't convinced that they would all be capable of using them if and when the need arose.

My real worry, however, was the day when we were due to throw hand grenades. This training was carried out in pairs, where we would be required to get into a trench, pull the pin and immediately hurl the grenade as far as possible up and over the sandbags. I was convinced from the outset that I would be allocated this function in company with the half-wit from the Virgin Islands, and that he would promptly pull the pin and drop it. Sure enough, there he was, next to me in the trench. I screamed to the sergeant in charge that this cretin was incapable of throwing a hand grenade responsibly, but was ignored. My wank-buddy was clearly nervous, fumbling with his grenade as if he'd never seen one before, apparently uncertain as to where to find the pin. All of a sudden, he found it, and before the sergeant could give the command, "Throw grenades", took the pin out, looked at the grenade thoughtfully for a moment – and promptly dropped it.

Whimpering, I scrabbled at the corner of the dugout, inca-pable of getting a grip and climbing out. At the same time, the sergeant, white as a sheet, acted in a manner that would have caused me to award him the Medal of Honor without a second thought. With commendable speed, he leapt into the pit, seized the grenade and hurled it, seconds before it exploded. My buddy was led away quietly, and I never saw him again. I hope at that point that the authorities finally became aware that he posed a greater threat to the US Army than he ever would have done to any prospective enemy.

In every other respect, I can say truthfully that I enjoyed much of the training, particularly when it was carried out indoors and in reasonable temperatures. Basic training held no real fears for me, having already served two years during my mid-teens in the

British Combined Cadet Force (CCF). Our sadistic sergeant-major at that time had proved far more horrific than anyone I later came across in the American forces. Likewise, slogging for miles with a 60lb pack on my back across the New Jersey countryside held no fears after compulsory school steeplechases. Discipline was reasonably strict but there was little evidence of direct bullying. The worst that could happen to you would be a requirement to, "Drop down and give me twenty-five", this being the normal number of push-ups expected to be attained in gymnastics by the end of the first eight weeks. These exercises, incidentally, were undertaken almost gratefully, carried outside in temperatures so cold that they provided a welcome opportunity to warm up. In those days, obesity was far rarer, and those slightly overweight soon found their waist receding to a healthier shape. I had, in fact, been slightly underweight when enlisting, and the obligation to drink a half pint of milk at every meal ensured that I actually gained 16lbs by the end of my basic training.

Most of us met the minimum standards with little difficulty, but one or two in the group, clearly revelling in their previous keep fit regimes, were way ahead of the rest, even at the outset. One lad left us all flabbergasted. Clearly a keep fit enthusiast *par excellence*, when the order was given to move to the bar (positioned about two feet above the head) and to raise his body so that his chin topped the bar, he stepped forward, swung himself into position like a monkey and proceeded to pull himself up and down tirelessly like a yo-yo. Surpassing the required twenty five, he delivered 30, 40, 50, and would clearly have been happy to go for the century, had the sergeant not told him to get down and stop showing off. With a smirk, he delivered the last two pull-ups with one hand, and dropped down.

I had become a reasonable shot with a Lee Enfield rifle

during my time in the CCF, and was eager to build on my shooting skills. By the end of basic training, I had qualified as 'expert' with the M1 rifle, carbine and sub-machine gun, to the point where I was later chosen to shoot for the US Seventh Army in an SMG competition. None of this, of course, was as much fun as shooting a Colt .45 pistol, and here we were all in fantasy land, prepared to take on the role of John Wayne or Clint Eastwood, where we would shoot from the hip and mow down our enemies before they could get a single shot off at us. We were crushed to discover that the effective range of a Colt .45 was about 20 yards (and even then you could only hope to hit an enemy if he were the size of Rosie Grier). Not only that, but one shot not from the hip but with arm extended vertically above the head, bringing the weapon down slowly to the horizontal position. This made us all feel like wimps; it wasn't the way Yul Bryner had done it in the *Magnificent Seven*, and we felt cheated.

Activities on the shooting range were the most fun. "Lock and load one round of ball ammunition" was the cry that kicked off a day's marksmanship fun. The cadre appeared to be less interested in our scoring bulls as our ability to group our shots. Why this should be the case, I never discovered. Why should a group of bullet holes in a tree adjacent to your enemy be deemed worthier than a couple of shots through his heart? The logic escaped me – but who was I, to search for logic in the thinking behind army training? The greatest crime, however, was failure to hit the target. A red flag – Maggie's drawers – would be raised and waved, to the jeers of other competitors and the despair of the marksman.

Once we were deemed to have satisfied the requirements of the fixed targets, we could move on to the obstacle course. Here, one was obliged to walk slowly along a defined pathway, casting glances to left and right, until – whey-hey! – a full-size cardboard figure would pop up. The shock of this sudden apparition was sufficient for some of us to drop our rifles or loose off a couple of misdirected rounds which threatened friendly-fire near-accidents. We were expected to get off one or two shots at it before it dropped out of sight again. The longer this process went on, the faster the figure dropped out of sight until the point was reached where you weren't quite certain whether the target had popped up at all, but blazed away happily at anything that moved, or appeared to move.

Once again, I was puzzled at why enemies would conveniently stand up in full view to challenge you, rather than simply potting you from behind a tree as you passed. Equally, why were the figures carrying cardboard weapons, but were themselves unable to loose off a shot at you? Perhaps their visage was thought suitably terrifying to scare you into submission and surrender without firing a shot. Looking more like low life from the Bronx or the baddies in Superman comics than enemy soldiers, they resembled no Soviet or other potential enemy trooper that I had ever seen pictured. I also felt that the nature of this particular pathway was such that no even halfway intelligent grunt would ever have dreamed of taking a stroll along it, faced as they were with the strong probability of being challenged by innumerable enemies lurking behind every boulder or tree.

CHAPTER 3

In which the Limey moves on to advanced training

At some point around this period, our company received a visit
from a US senator, whose name (fortunately, for his sake) now
escapes me. Quite what these senators expect to achieve, by
visiting troops on training and playing the role of a visiting dig-
nitary, is unclear. It was expressed to us as an exercise to boost
morale – but whether ours or the senator's is anybody's guess.
Anyway, I happened to be in the front line of the assembled
troops, and as luck would have it, the senator decided to stop
and have a word with me.

"And where are you from, young man?" he enquired.

"From London, sir," I replied.

"Ah, good to welcome you Irish over here." He smiled and
passed on, and I watched the accompanying officer's eyes rise to
the sky in silent appeal.

Towards the end of our training, we were shown official
training films which had been put together (extraordinarily
badly) by a military film unit. Most were boring beyond belief,
but the welcome darkness allowed us to switch off and doze,
unaware or uncaring that the failure to imbibe these vital tips
undermined the whole freedom of our glorious United States.

One film, however, made us waken with a start – it depicted battlefield wounds and how to dispense First Aid in the field. I remember vividly sucking chest wounds in glorious technicolour, and the impact these scenes had on my fellow GIs. Even in the dark I could see their pallid faces whitening, and one or two felt obliged to head for the latrines.

Before criticising US Army films too extensively, I should add that far worse features were those made by the British Army's film unit which, in the US military's wisdom, they had thought would be useful to show us. One film selected involved night manoeuvres. A group of English squaddies were apparently undertaking a night field exercise, which of course took place in total darkness. This grainy black and white film (which I judged could have been put together some twenty or thirty years previously) was more black than white, with most of the action entailing nothing beyond an occasional shape looming out of the gloom, exchanging a few words of command with another and disappearing again into the blackness. What made it worse was that the troops selected were all drawn from Geordie volunteers whose accent was incomprehensible not only to the other GIs but also to me.

"What the hell are these guys on about, Limey?" whispered a lad next to me, and I had to confess I hadn't understood a word.

Apart from the compulsion to drink endless pints of milk, US Army meals, served on traditional six-part metal trays were not only filling but quite satisfying too. I remember healthy breakfasts consisting of several thousand calories and a lot of chicken and corn for main meals, well cooked and tasty enough. An unpopular but obviously low-cost meal was chipped beef in a kind of cream sauce, known universally as SOS (Shit On Shingle), but even this I found infinitely preferable to meals I had been served at school and on visits to military establishments in the UK in my former life. In fact, I was quite happy with what I was eating, until the pleasures of pulling my first KP (kitchen police) duties, in which food preparation and kitchen cleaning became an essential chore at some point in the training programme (wonderfully, this chore disappeared once I was assigned overseas, as local civilians were employed to undertake these tasks. This privilege made me feel like a member of an army of occupation).

Although hard work, food preparation was not an objectionable occupation – but the cleaning was. The least attractive chore was cleaning out the filth from the grease trap, which meant raising the grid in the centre of the kitchen and scooping out with one's hands as much as possible of the grease and dirt that had accumulated there over the previous few days. The chefs, all career soldiers of massive dimensions and from the deep South, were hard taskmasters, and I was thankful to have had to pull this duty only a couple of times during my basic training days.

Entertainment during our leisure hours was limited to a rather seedy bar on base (no one was authorised to leave the base in the first eight weeks) where we drank '2.4', a weak lager (the number alluded to the alcohol content) which Americans refer to as 'lawnmower beer', suggesting its suitability to quench one's thirst after heavy gardening duty. The consumption of at least ten pints was necessary before we could notice any effect whatsoever. This ploy was a neat means of furthering the bar's profits, on top of those already assured as a closed shop monopoly. If the intention was to reduce drunkenness, it was an unsuccessful ruse because we simply set about drinking more as quickly as possible to obtain the required level of inebriation. However, the amount needed to become violent or aggressive would require a level of drinking so daunting that few would have achieved this state, so unpleasantness was limited.

47

* * *

Upon completion of the first eight weeks, we were assigned to new companies to complete our advanced training. In some cases, this meant leaving Dix and transferring to other camps scattered around the country. I was to remain at Fort Dix, assigned to a clerk-typist programme, so completed my training in familiar territory. Before launching into this, however, we were to be granted our first weekend pass.

What a joy to be back in New York again after the trials and tribulations of eight weeks' basic! Although on my own, I was happy to wander along Broadway and through Times Square, taking in the sights and the bright lights, enjoying proper food and beer (bliss!). I even ended up at Roseland, then a rather run down dance hall where, to my delight, Gene Krupa was playing the drums in his declining, drug-addled years. His performing ability, however, showed no signs of diminishing. For the price of a one-dollar drink I could stand six feet away from the greatest drummer of all time, in company with fewer than a dozen other fans, and listen to him play all night. Nobody seemed concerned about whether I ordered another beer, or indeed whether I drank at all. I couldn't believe my luck.

The weekend passed all too quickly. Sunday evening saw me catching one of the last Greyhound buses back to Fort Dix, where I arrived during the worst storm I was ever to experience in my life. Alighting from the bus in Fort Dix, I found myself up to my ankles in flood water, while frequent flashes of lightning lit up the sky with an intensity that made it hard to believe that darkness had fallen more than two hours earlier. The rain not so much fell as appeared to have been tipped out of a bath, descending in a cascade which soaked me to the skin within seconds. My mood changed quickly from elation to depression as I faced up to another eight weeks of mid-winter in the backwoods, with an uncertain military future.

However, the second half of my training, while strenuous, held none of the fears experienced during basic training. More time was spent in well-heated barracks with classroom hours devoted to mastering typewriting. It was a slog, but one for which I am eternally grateful, giving me the use of ten fingers when computers came along, rather than the more common two employed by my fellow workers. As I recall, most of these classroom hours were dedicated to learning how to complete the MORNING REPORT (it was always spoken of in capital letters, and with immense gravitas, eliding the term as if a single word).

The MORNING REPORT, it was stressed time and again, was by far the single most important document issued by the military; more important than any simple requisitions for military equipment, regardless of the billions invested. These reports had to be typed by the clerk responsible not just neatly but immaculately. Mere typing errors, we were advised, were deemed sufficient to ensure the miserable grunt responsible would be incarcerated at Fort Leavenworth military prison for a minimum of ten years, while more serious errors or omissions would guarantee the death penalty in most States. In consequence, stress levels were high during these periods of training, and our failure rate in this key document was far higher than in other forms we were trained to complete. It didn't help that the completion of the MORNING REPORT had to employ military terminology which bore little resemblance to any normal phraseology found in the English language – this was a skill that I never adequately mastered.

A speed of at least 60 words per minute was deemed the minimum standard to achieve in order to move on to the more glorified opportunities in the military white collar world, designating the individual as a clerk-typist, while speeds of 30-60 wpm would doom one to more boring, sedentary occupations as a humble general clerk, specialty number 710.00. At the end of my period of training, I was presented with a splendid sheet of parchment informing me that I had successfully completed a Basic Army Administration Course, MOS 710.0, and was thus entitled to transfer to a full time posting in a lowly clerical capacity anywhere on the planet where the US Government had at that time decided to keep the peace. This, however, was far from my sole achievement. It appeared that, unbeknown to me, I had managed to complete a whole series of esoteric and challenging courses, including that of a driver competent to drive a standard Willys army jeep with trailer, and (more curiously) an ability to perform the duties of a hot water warm air furnace engineer. What training I was given to perform these pursuits has escaped me, but doubtless would be called back into memory were I ever to be faced by an enemy threatening to sabotage the central heating system in my trench.

In fact, driving a jeep with trailer attached is far more challenging than one might suppose. Having held a driving licence for all of five years, I thought driving a jeep would be a doddle.

This was far from the case. Not only did jeeps have sensitive chokes which had to be pulled out to exactly the right extent in order to fire the engine without stalling it, but they were also equipped with a dual drive two- or four-wheel transmission which, in my case at least, seemed to have a mind of its own.

The biggest challenge, however, was learning to reverse a jeep fitted with a trailer. Against all the laws of logic, one must turn the steering wheel in the opposite direction to that in which you want the trailer to go. Any sharp movement has the interesting effect of jack-knifing both vehicles (a process which locks trailer and jeep together irredeemably) until you can round up a couple of buddies to come along and bounce the trailer up and down a few times to dislodge it from its attempt to climb over the rear seat.

On the straight, the task is hard enough, but on manoeuvres, in muddy terrain where the vehicle may be parked at an angle of 50 or 60 degrees on the side of a hill, the task becomes superhuman. It certainly passed my worst driving memory up to that point, which had been taking my driving test during the rush hour in London, in which I was obliged to drive through the main street in Croydon with one side of the street dug up, attempting to squeeze between on-coming double-decker buses and a crowded pavement. At times this forced me to mount the kerb and almost obliterate a stream of Saturday morning shoppers. Glancing into my rear view mirror as I returned to the road, my lasting memory was of distracted shoppers, mouths agape, eyes wide with terror, flattening themselves against the shops' display windows. Somehow, the driving examiner took pity on me and I scraped through the test.

So, suitably armed with our barrage of qualifications, and revelling in our first promotion from Private E-1 to Private E-2 (accompanied by a modest rise in salary) we waited to hear our fate. At the time, most troops undertaking their period of national service were dispatched to AFFE (American Forces Far East, which essentially meant South Korea). The Korean War was long over, but US troops continued to patrol the border between North and South, and rumours that had percolated back indicated that this was an experience to be avoided where possible. Temperatures were even more extreme than those experienced at Fort Dix and facilities were primitive. Activity was limited to marching up and down the border, watching for infiltrators in company with ROK (Republic of Korea) troops whose English was limited and whose dislike of American forces was only marginally less than that of the North Koreans.

I needed to avoid this experience at all costs, and requested compassionate assignment, on the grounds that my elderly (just turned 60) and medically unfit (they were both fine, as far as I knew) parents needed me near them, and I had promised to get over to help them when necessary. A sympathetic officer heard my plea and assigned me to Germany. Mine was the lone European assignment; the rest of the poor sods were assigned to AFFE.

Thus I found myself, one warm spring day in 1957, on my way to McGuire Air Force Base, New Jersey, whence I was to catch a MATS (Military Air Transport Service) aircraft bound for Frankfurt.

CHAPTER 4

In which the Limey joins the US Seventh Army in Germany

My relief at having successfully completed the first sixteen weeks of training was short-lived. I eyed the aircraft awaiting us on the runway with apprehension. MATS carried members of the armed forces around the world, and given that these were not civilians paying their own way and demanding a certain degree of comfort and service, I wasn't expecting the last word in aviation technology. In any case, jet aircraft were a recent novelty, and I was resigned to travelling in propeller aircraft which had seen service in Korea and elsewhere.

What I hadn't anticipated was a four-engine propeller aircraft which looked like it might have served in World War II on bombing raids over Germany, and possibly been hit by anti-aircraft flak on several occasions. The darkness of the night sky, with no sign of a moon, hid some of the greater deficiencies as we walked out onto the tarmac, climbed in some trepidation into the bowels of the aircraft, and took our seats.

Comfort was not the first consideration of MATS personnel when sourcing their equipment, and these seats had thin upholstery through which the hard metal frame could clearly be felt. This did not bode well for a long flight, but at least I was aware that the range of these aircraft was limited, obliging us to come down at least twice on our route across the Atlantic in order to refuel. My greater worry was that our descents could turn out to be more frequent than programmed and possibly not even over dry land.

The pilot seemed to be in a hurry, whether to get back to Germany to meet up with his girlfriend or to deliver his aircraft with its two hundred souls safely and in one piece before the whole contraption fell out of the sky, we couldn't be certain. In any event, hardly had we settled back in our seats when the engines burst into a throaty roar and we were careering down the runway – at which point the near port engine promptly burst into flames.

I occupied a window seat on the port side, and so had a grandstand view of this event. As flames shot out of the rear of the engine, with a roar which almost drowned our screams of terror, the pilot must have also taken note of the crisis. Slamming on the brakes, he shut down the engines and aborted the take-off. We skidded to a halt.

Thinking this would lead to a lay-over, and a delay of at least a few hours, I was pleased to think we might get a chance to recover our shattered nerves. But no. We were immediately transferred onto another aircraft and the cargo of extremely disturbed troopers was on its way again in a matter of minutes.

Our first port of call was Gander, Newfoundland, then an important base for the US Air Force during the Cold War. My sympathies were with the poor, frozen airmen stationed at this god-forsaken outpost which had little to offer in the way of recreation. There was nowhere to go if you went off-base – unless rubbing noses with an Inuit was your idea of passing an enjoyable afternoon.

I had thought the terror of being in the air in a 1940s crate held together with string and wallpaper paste was the worst way one could imagine of passing a few hours, but found this superseded by the sheer boredom of sitting in a Nissen Hut listening to the wind and snow howling around the buildings, while posters on every wall reminded me of the pleasurable adventures I could look forward to, were I to choose to re-enlist in the armed forces for a further three years. It was almost a relief to take up our seats again in the aircraft, now bound for Prestwick, Scotland.

It was a strange experience, landing again in one's own country wearing the uniform of the armed services of a foreign land. I once again wondered idly what would be the legal consequences if I were to make a break for it, climb out of a toilet window and head back to London. Would the British allow the extradition of one of their own citizens for going AWOL from a foreign army while in their own country? Would the American authorities bother with an extradition? (I've never resolved these questions.)

In any event, good sense took over and, remembering that my long-term plans included the hope of returning to the States and working there in due course, I climbed back onto the aircraft with the rest of my colleagues and settled down for the final lap of the journey into Frankfurt-on-Main.

Rhein-Main Airport was at that time a major hub for both civilian and US military air movements, occupying a huge tract of land. This was, in the event, my first visit to Germany. Given that all my knowledge and attitudes towards the country had been shaped as a child by my experiences and memories of war, I was eager to learn about it at first hand. Here we were to be 'processed' for a couple of days pending transfer to our individual ultimate assignments. *Inter alia*, processing involved indoctrination into the German way of life and lectures on what would be expected of us in our dealings with the natives, together with another round of comical training films.

Today I can only recall the latter. Filled with unconscious humour, they remain among my most treasured memories of army life. My particular favourite followed the story of a young soldier from the mid-West experiencing his first visit to town. Naïve to the point of gormlessness, but nevertheless immaculate in freshly pressed uniform and sporting a remarkable number of decorations for a soldier purporting to be on his first foreign posting, our hero was accosted from every alleyway and portal as he made his way from bus station to town centre. Those accosting were unfailingly gorgeous – long-legged, attractively cleavaged, with pouting lips and dancing eyes (we imagined they were unemployed Hollywood starlets taking up any available bit parts), they exercised all their guile and feminine wiles to entrap this paragon of virtue but, lantern-jawed, he remained steadfast and immune to all appeals.

Meanwhile we were dividing our time ogling the screen while trying to identify the streets where these delights were to be located, and making scribbled notes on the backs of envelopes of any clues, in the form of hotel or bar names, which might help us to narrow our search. Throughout, the voice-over was telling us, in stern tones, that this particular pleasure was not for us. Shortly, our hero found himself on a bridge, where he soon got into conversation with a no less attractive but more modestly attired young lady. Clean-cut, evidently highly educated and from a good family, she appeared to have every conceivable virtue apart, perhaps, from an apparent willingness to engage in conversation at the drop of a hat with any low-life, ill-paid foreigner she encountered, as long as they appeared reasonably well-dressed. Within minutes, it seemed, she had elicited the facts that he was alone at Christmas, eager to get to know the locals and of honest intentions – so promptly invited him home to spend Christmas with the family.

My goodness, had this guy struck lucky! Not only did the family live in a turreted mansion resembling a fairytale castle, but Daddy turned out to be the local baron. Dinner was served by uniformed servants in a baronial hall, below crystal chandeliers, with silver candlesticks and cutlery on the table. The guests appeared to number around fourteen, all seated around a magnificent mediaeval banqueting table. Everyone spoke fluent English with scarcely a trace of German accent, and engaged our hero in intellectual and stimulating conversation about life in Germany and America.

What intrigued us, however, was the fact that – following the carving up of the single turkey – each guest had managed to end up with a leg!

We looked back at the carving table again. No, there was just one bird, admittedly enormous though now reduced to a skeleton; but there could be no doubt, the silver platter bore but one. Whether this represented some rare breed of German poultry of which we knew nothing, or merely testified to appalling continuity, we were at a loss to know, but without exception we found it all highly entertaining, while the voice-over continued with a soothing commentary suggesting that such rewards awaited all of us, if only we were to conduct ourselves in an appropriate manner when out on weekend passes.

During our brief stopover in Frankfurt we were at liberty to go into town during the evening and I made full use of the opportunity. Marshall aid was obviously making a great impression here and the substantially rebuilt city glowed with light – quite a contrast to towns of similar size in Britain at that time.

Inevitably finding my way to the seamier streets of the city I was unsurprised to find, loitering in the entrance ways, all the pleasurable opportunities about which the training films had warned us just 24 hours earlier. However, closer examination revealed that none of these were out of work Hollywood actresses, but rather some distinctly plain, and by no means young, women whose knowledge of the English language was limited to a request for cigarettes and a few well-chosen and easily communicated Anglo-Saxon expressions. At this point, I found it easy enough to take on the role of the film hero and continued my quest for the baron's daughter. By eleven o'clock, unwilling to face the risk of becoming AWOL, I had to admit defeat, and returned to my temporary barracks.

My orders had identified my eventual destination as 'schwetz'gen'. I had documents providing me with transport to Heidelberg Railway Station where I was met by a surly and abrasively disposed corporal with a jeep. I discovered my base was to be Tompkins Barracks in Schwetzingen, a rather pretty small town (little more than a village in those days) some ten miles from Heidelberg itself, the base for US Army Headquarters in Europe. As a consequence, the area was saturated with US military establishments including Patrick Henry Village on the outskirts of Heidelberg – quarters for the civilian families of members of the armed forces and understood to be the largest American installation outside the US mainland.

Heidelberg itself was then a charming town – already a well-established tourist destination and world-renowned for its castle and mediaeval bridge across the River Neckar. It had sustained little obvious damage during the war, and was yet to suffer the ravages of post-war development that would so mar the town in the later 1960s and 1970s (although its popularity on the tourist trail has never diminished). Its narrow main street, the Hauptstrasse, was at that time unpedestrianised, lined with elegant shops, bars and restaurants and transited by one of the

FIG 2 Haupstrasse, Heidelberg, Summer 1957.

many blue and white streetcar routes serving the area. As a result, crossing the road meant serious risk to life and limb.

It had been a puzzle to me why more American servicemen did not return to their country in a box after imbibing too liberally the German lagers (far stronger than those which they were used to back home) before stepping off unthinkingly onto the tramlines to cross this narrow road. I can only ascribe their survival to the training and quick wit of the German streetcar drivers, long familiar with this particular threat to their careers. I can recall at least two occasions on which I nearly came to grief myself (only one of which can be ascribed to alcohol consumption – the other resulted from my being distracted by the appearance of an attractive blonde on the pavement opposite).

The pedestrianisation of the Hauptstrasse occurred some time after I completed my army service and it is one of the very few examples I can think of where the scheme simply hasn't worked. It didn't help that its execution was carried out so poorly, with little or no planting or street furniture to modify the acres of concrete paving. I can remember my disappointment on my first return to the city some years later, at how much of its charm had been lost in the intervening years.

Schwetzingen was another matter. It boasted a castle (site of the annual international music festival which remains the high point of the town's year) and a rather attractive small square with restaurants and bars. At that time Schwetzingen was a sleepy little place, offering little to attract the troops based at the nearby barracks who would prefer, on their weekend passes, to spend their time travelling by streetcar into Heidelberg where they could enjoy the lively shops and nightlife.

Tompkins was a small barracks just a short walk from the village. Formerly a base occupied by a German Panzer unit throughout World War II, it consisted of six rather fine, solidly

FIG 3 Entertainment on base. I'm a candidate on the $64,000 Question (the actual payout was somewhat less).

constructed buildings set around a quadrangle and designed in the popular style of their day which might loosely be termed Teutonic Gothic. Small turrets sprouted liberally from the rooftops, and entrances were marked by the kind of doorways one would normally expect to see on entering the Reichskanzlerei – minus bomb damage. Facilities were good, with bedrooms accommodating just six or eight soldiers and good public rooms – an entertainments area with easy chairs, and a rather unattractive bar just outside the campus separated into facilities for officers, NCOs and other ranks.

I spent only one evening here, and came home to my room so depressed by the experience that I never went again. How any inductees could choose to do their drinking in such depressing surroundings when a short streetcar ride away they could enjoy the bonhomie of a German bar escaped me. In fact not many did so choose. The bar's custom largely depended upon career NCOs who preferred American 'lawnmower' beer to the superior stuff served 'on the economy'.

One other facility was an annexe to the barracks which accommodated some elements of the German forces. Surprisingly, given that the war had been over for more than a dozen years by then, these soldiers still provided many basic services for the US troopers, and for a small sum could be encouraged to clean and repair boots or fulfil other useful small services which Americans seemed to treat as beneath their dignity to take on. German civilians also did all the cooking, cleaning and KP work, so that in truth life in the US Army in these early post-occupation years was by no means unpleasant.

Our earnings, even as a basic trooper, subsidised by overseas allowances, provided us with an income sufficient to enjoy eating and drinking in the finest watering holes in Heidelberg, and I recall with fondness my meals at the five star Hotel Europahof, where I would sit on Saturday evenings devouring saddle of venison with a fine wine to accompany it, watched enviously (and in some cases with open hostility) by German businessmen. Regular army NCOs were earning so much that they could afford to live like kings, and the car park at the barracks was filled with the latest Mercedes and Porsches that would in due course rotate with them back to their home in the USA when their tour of duty in Germany was completed. By then, they wouldn't even have attracted import duties, being classed as used vehicles.

This is in sad contrast to the circumstances in which soldiers based in those same barracks find themselves today. The German economy has prospered at the expense of the American, and

Fig 4 Tompkins Barracks, Schwetzingen.

FIG 5 Full parade at Tompkins, summer 1958.

FIG 6 (top) At Tompkins Barracks, Schwetzingen, Germany, Summer 1958.
FIG 7 (above) On board USS Geiger on a rare sunny day, December 1958.

FIG 8 (above) Awaiting separation at Fort Dix, NJ, January 1959.
FIG 9 (top) Shortly before separation at Fort Dix, January 1959.

army salaries have failed to keep pace with local costs, with the result that on a visit made many years later I found those stationed here (almost without exception poor African-Americans from Southern States serving as members of the regular forces, conscription having long been phased out) to be so impoverished that they seldom ventured far from their own facilities.

My last visit followed soon after the tragedy of the September 11 2001 attack on New York's twin towers. Security was at its maximum and I could not gain access beyond the main gate. As it was, our car undercarriage was screened with mirrors and we were regarded with suspicion by the duty guard for even wishing to consider entering the base. He plainly didn't believe me when I showed him my British passport, and told him I had served as a member of the US armed forces there over forty years earlier.

CHAPTER 5

In which the Limey learns all about the American Way of Life, and is rewarded with the best job in the army

Any sociologist given the chance to study the US Army in the late 1950s would find a wealth of fascinating data. No doubt some did, since they would have faced conscription along with other graduates at the end of their university courses (unless they could delay the inevitable by continuing to study until they had passed their twenty-sixth birthday, thus exempting them from conscription).

Levels of intelligence seemed to be in inverse proportion to the ranks held. Many of the young privates conscripted to serve with me at Tompkins were graduates from leading Ivy League universities (one, who served with me as company clerk and later went on to become a leading corporate lawyer in Boston, was a recent graduate with honours from Harvard and hailed from a well-connected Boston family). By contrast, the officers had often attended undistinguished military academies and emerged with distinctly unimpressive records, to the extent that many of us were seriously worried about the prospect of having to serve under them if called upon to see active service. It came as no surprise to me when, years later, I read of the practice of 'fragging' in Vietnam – or blowing up your own officers with hand grenades to avoid following orders which enlisted men deemed suicidal.

On arrival at Tompkins, my driver delivered me safely to my barracks. I was instructed to report to the company commanding officer, a young second lieutenant on his first command assignment. My company, HQ Co, 11th Engineer Group, was designed primarily to fulfil administrative roles and I was assigned to become mailman for the group to replace the current incumbent who was due to rotate a couple of weeks later.

The conversation with my CO was brief and formal. I had the distinct impression that he'd had his feet up on the desk at the moment when I entered his office, and disliked being disturbed during his afternoon nap. He showed no interest in me as a person, merely following SOP (standard operating procedure) by welcoming me and directing me on my duties.

Obviously anxious to dismiss me, he barked, "Any questions?"

"Just one, Sir," I replied. "Is there a Goethe Haus in town?"

This institution organised cultural exchanges between Germans and visitors to the country. Among other activities they arranged to conduct German language classes, which I was keen to follow.

My CO looked at me blankly. "What the hell's that?" he enquired.

I explained to him patiently the role of the Goethe Haus. He clearly thought I was mad to want to bother to learn any language, and suggested I made enquiries in Heidelberg. It was my first and last personal meeting with him.

Having been assigned to the mailroom, I lost no time in acquainting myself with my duties there. The present incumbent was helpful in breaking me in, explaining that I had landed the cushiest job in the army (with the possible exception of the Chaplain's Assistant – but for that, you need to play the organ). "You get assigned your own jeep and drive each morning to the Army Post Office in Heidelberg where you draw mail for the barracks," he said. "You return before lunchtime and open the post office for an hour to allow the troops to visit and collect their mail. This gets you out of the morning parade and a lot of other bullshit. You then drive back again in the afternoon and get the late mail, returning to the barracks in time to open the office for a further hour, escaping any other dogsbody jobs that you might have been assigned to if you hung around here. You then knock off for the evening meal."

This sounded like paradise, and when I found that I might on occasion also be called upon to deliver confidential (even top secret) documents, for which occasions I was required to draw a Colt .45 pistol and eight rounds of live ammunition with orders to shoot anyone who marred my progress, I was in seventh heaven.

The current mail clerk, Bormann, was a tall, good-looking and intelligent man from New Jersey. As his name would indicate, he came from German stock and in fact had quite a good understanding of the language which stood him in good stead when driving into town for the morning mail – a duty on which I accompanied him for his last two weeks. He was a ferocious, if able, driver, and clearly felt that the importance of his role took precedence over that of any other vehicle on the road. This led to frequent altercations in the narrow streets of Heidelberg, where Bormann would use his choice selection of German abuse to good effect. I can still recall his shout of "*Sei nicht so frech!*" directed at locals running in front of his vehicle when crossing the road, using the familiar German term for 'you' regardless of their age and status. Locals were so surprised to hear any

American soldiers addressing them in their own language that they seldom chose to argue, so our passage was invariably speedy, allowing us more time to meander around the town and do a spot of shopping before driving slowly back to the barracks in time for the noon postal service.

US Army postal regulations were contained in a substantial instruction manual which I was supposed to have read and digested as soon as I took up my role. It instructed me on how to maintain the office, the hours at which I had to open and close, precautions against theft and burglary and detailed the necessary tools of the trade for weighing and franking letters and parcels which I was obliged to protect. It also alerted me to a regulation which was less welcome – that the position to which I had been entrusted was one that could be held only by a US citizen, whether native or naturalised. I was neither. On the other hand I was in a cushy job, and since nobody else appeared to have read the regulations or to have picked up this particular discrepancy, I wasn't about to bring it to anyone's notice. I got away with this almost to the end of my period of service (about which, more later).

Of course, procedures as they stood were far too attractive to survive for long. The need to travel twice a day into Heidelberg to collect mail was clearly superfluous, but somehow Bormann had got away with it throughout his national service. Shortly after his departure, however, some bright spark realised that I was returning with as few as two or three letters in the afternoon, and felt that I could be doing something more useful. Thus, the afternoon mail run was discontinued, and I had to turn up to some of the routine activities undertaken by my fellow-soldiers.

In some ways this turned out to be a blessing in disguise, as assemblies became the occasion for much hilarity. Parades were overseen by the NCO in charge, a Master Sergeant. MSgt

FIG 10 My jeep, ready to roll on the morning mail run.

Koschmeier was florid-faced, over-weight and greatly out of condition, and a man of such limited intellect that it escaped us how he could have survived so long in any capacity in the army – even in an army as unfussy about whom it recruited as this one. One example will suffice. At assembly, a roll call was taken of all troops expected to attend, and on one occasion this cretin actually called out his own name, waited briefly for a response, then added, "Oh, that's me".

It sobered me to think that we were supposed to entrust our lives to him, if called upon to do so.

Among the troops in HQ Co was a young soldier who had originated from Poland, name of Mancewicz. Somehow Mancewicz had escaped from his Soviet-occupied country and made his way to the United States, where he had found work and contentment, ultimately enlisting in the army. For Mancewicz, the USA stood for everything that was good in the world. He revelled in its liberty, its individualism, its can-do mentality. What's more, he took the idea of democracy, and the rights this provided, very seriously. Upon joining the army, he took it upon himself to read, master and apparently commit to memory the entire contents of the UCMJ (Uniform Code of Military Justice), a massive tome covering hundreds of pages of small print outlining the freedoms and obligations of the armed forces. It was the rights that interested him most.

He would decide to fight for these at inconvenient moments, and most commonly during morning assemblies, at the exact moment when Koschmeier had started to take the roll call. The good sergeant would be abruptly interrupted in full flow by a cry from Mancewicz, "One moment, Sergeant.... I have a question."

The MSgt stopped, and rolled his eyes to the heavens. "Shut up, Mancewicz, I'm taking roll call."

The good Pole would become excitable and insistent, "I regret I cannot shut up, Sergeant, I have a right. I have a right under the Uniform Code of Military Justice, section X sub-section Y, paragraph Z, to ask a question."

The sergeant pondered upon this for a moment, then, deciding this was not an appropriate moment to get into a full scale argument about the boundaries of military freedom of expression, gave way. "Oh, all right, Mancewicz," he sighed. "Get on with it."

For the next ten minutes Mancewicz would follow some obscure issue regarding an infringement of his rights which none of us could make head or tail of, but which was the cause of enormous merriment. We all took this good-naturedly, even though it invariably delayed the completion of our morning assemblies by several minutes.

Koschmeier had somehow managed to get himself engaged to one of the prettiest girls in town, which should have kept him happy. But as time passed and his rotation approached, he showed signs of depression. He explained to a colleague that he couldn't understand why it was taking him so long to acquire permission to marry, and thus a visa for his girlfriend to accompany him back to the States at the end of his assignment. We didn't feel it would be kind to notify him that, not only was his girlfriend the most notable prostitute in town, her father also happened to be a prominent member of the local Communist Party. I don't think poor Koschmeier ever did find out the truth, eventually rotating alone, no doubt to give much further amusement to other troopers back in the USA.

An equally colourful character was our adjutant, a certain Major Rohan. This was a time when non-graduate serving officers were under pressure to obtain degree qualifications, in a drive by the army to bring all officer ranks up to degree standard. As this was an essential criterion for promotion, most tried to enrol to complete a degree on a part-time basis. Rohan was one of many officers who decided that the simplest means by which he could gain himself an education would be to enrol in a distance learning degree offered by the University of Maryland. This was essentially a correspondence course, obliging the candidates to undertake some simple reading, following which they were required to write a piece of coursework which was then submitted by mail to the University each week.

After struggling with the first assignment for several hours, Rohan strode into the office and hurled the assignment on the desk of the company clerk, our Harvard-educated legal eagle. "Here, I can't make head or tail of this. Take care of it for me, will you?"

And Marvin, good private that he was, did so, eventually

getting him through the programme and his degree award. Certainly, there would have been little prospect of the good Major achieving this without his clerk's help.

Up to this point my army driving licence equipped me only to drive jeeps or similar light vehicles, but evidently everyone assigned to this HQ unit was expected at very least to be capable of driving a two and a half ton truck, known affectionately as a 'deuce and a half'. Soon after my arrival, I was called out to report to the motor pool sergeant, where I was told that I would be taking the test. The idea of some training up front had evidently not occurred to them, and anyway, if anything got in the way on the road, the truck would probably have come off best. So without more ado I was instructed to climb into the driving seat, the good sergeant alongside.

The gears were basic, but familiar enough, and the brake and clutch, while out of reach, were at least in the right place. I found that by slumping in my seat and thrusting my foot forward as far as it would reach, I could just about hit the brake. This unfortunately had the effect of bringing my eyes down to the level of the dashboard, but by straining my neck, I found I could just see the tops of oncoming vehicles above the hood (bonnet to you and me). Thus reassured, I engaged the gear, and set off.

I thought I'd play it safe to start with, and kept to a steady two miles an hour, gradually increasing this to 5 mph when we emerged onto the main road. The sergeant glanced at me, looking unexpectedly tense, but said little beyond instructing me which routes to take. The entire driving test took up fewer than fifteen minutes. My performance would have any driving instructor in Britain pulling me over to the side of the road before I had gone a hundred yards and asking me where I had learned to drive. But for the purposes of the US Army I was apparently deemed proficient, and somehow got the vehicle back to the motor pool without either sideswiping any parked civilian vehicles en route or writing off any army vehicles on the base.

I got my licence but in fact never had cause to drive this particular type of vehicle again (for which I was eternally grateful) apart from one brief occasion when on manoeuvres. Somebody unaware of my particular talents in driving heavy vehicles assigned me to a deuce and a half *with trailer*, which I was required to back up on a steep-ish incline before I set off. Of course I promptly jack-knifed – I prefer to draw a veil over the subsequent humiliation, but suffice to say I never got called upon to take one out again.

I soon settled in to my barracks room, in company with five other enlisted men. These were a fascinating mix, mainly conscripted, but two of my room mates were regular army. What was more extraordinary, one was English – and so English that he would have been judged a caricature even in his own country. Oxford-educated, stiff-upper-lipped, with a cut-glass English accent and Brylcreemed hair, he appeared like a fish out of water in these surroundings and was, of course, ragged mercilessly. He was reserved, and spoke little about his life before enlisting. I never found out what he was doing in the States or why he had volunteered for service in the US Army.

No one in the room had much in common, not even geographically, with homes ranging from Little Rock, Arkansas to Chicago, Illinois. Bob came from a wealthy New England family background and gave the impression that this entitled him to advantages denied to others. His clothes cupboard was always stacked full with purchases, ignoring the usual limits on personal items, and he paid scant attention to the standing requirement to maintain this cupboard in pristine condition at all times.

As luck would have it, Bob was on leave at the time an IG

(Inspection General) was called, and all cupboards were required to be opened for inspection. We stood stiffly to attention in front of our cupboards and lockers, each with its door open. Bob's remained firmly closed. The inspecting officer asked the duty sergeant to find a key to open the doors, and after a short interval the sergeant returned with a master key. Knowing the state of Bob's equipment, we watched the cupboard in anguished trepidation. The sergeant seemed to have some difficulty in turning the lock.

We helpfully suggested he press against the door as he turned the key. He did so and the lock turned...

I was reminded of the famous scene in the Marx Brothers film in which a cabin door on their transatlantic liner bursts open to disgorge a pile of humans and baggage into the corridor. The explosion from Bob's cupboard was no less catastrophic; stuffed from top to bottom with packages of every conceivable size and shape, the contents exploded across the floor, knocking both sergeant and officer back against the bed. We desperately fought to keep straight faces.

The sergeant was apoplectic with fury. "Get this cleaned up!" he yelled at no one in particular, and strode from the barracks.

How this calamity affected the grading for the inspection we had no means of knowing, but I recall that the sergeant had lost none of his fury by the time Bob returned two weeks later, and he was grounded.

Bob was not short of the readies and soon after his arrival, he went out to purchase a brand new Porsche 911. Not content with its initial performance, he proceeded to strip out most of the interior (including the rear bucket seats) to lighten it, then he and I went off for the day to try it out. The obvious place to do this was at the Hockenheim Ring, an international motor racing circuit nearby. The place was deserted when we arrived and we managed to get the vehicle onto the track without difficulty. Bob gave it a couple of spins and declared himself satisfied, then asked if I'd like a go. I was only too happy. The fact that I'd never driven a sports car before, let alone what amounted now to a racing car, was lost on me, and I set off with my foot flat down on the accelerator. The car spun sharply, executed three turns and landed in the grassed area at the side of the track where it ploughed a trench six inches deep before I was able to cut the engine. Bob came over, looking concerned (perhaps more so for the car than what might have happened to me), but fortunately the vehicle had sustained only light damage and was soon back in running order. However, I decided to make this my last experience in motor racing, and got a lot of stick from the others when the story leaked out.

Among the NCOs present was one who was older and appeared to command greater respect from fellow NCOs than would normally be accorded to colleagues. It took us a while to find out why this was. There is a curious regulation in the US Army that requires officers to achieve promotion to a higher rank on a regular basis, and within a given number of years. Should they not do so, for example should their 'category run out' in army terminology, they would normally be expected to retire from the armed forces. But should they wish to remain, they would have to accept a reduction in rank to that of an NCO. This particular officer loved the army and couldn't envisage any other kind of career, so he elected to remain in the force as a three stripe sergeant.

While he seemed perfectly happy to accept the demotion, his wife wasn't. Her loss of face when told she would have to accompany her husband to the sergeants' mess rather than the officers' proved a step too far. Moreover, she was evidently shunned by those officers' wives whom she formerly counted as friends, and the ignominy was too much for her. She divorced her husband. Heigh-ho! Evidently snobbery in the US forces is as great, at least in some situations, as that one is led to believe is traditional in the British armed services.

The drive to improve the general education of the US armed forces was not limited to raising commissioned officers to degree standard. Many regular troops in the 1950s were from very poorly educated backgrounds, even in some cases lacking the basic ability to read and write. Among many poor families, the army was often seen as a good means to achieve advancement in life and a regular income, with parents encouraging their children to sign on as soon as they came of age. We had one such individual in our unit who delighted in the gloriously exotic name of Gwenneth Fillingame, and who worked as a mechanic in the motor pool. A charming, quiet and well-mannered lad, his literacy was limited to an ability to write his own name. However in this he excelled and after much practice became capable of producing a signature in superb copperplate lettering that would have been the envy of John Hancock himself. The irony was that he was the best mechanic the unit had. Capable of field stripping a jeep and putting it together again in a matter of minutes, he could turn his hand to the repair of any vehicle in the motor pool. This was undoubtedly the kind of soldier you wanted alongside you when under fire. Yet the army, in its wisdom, decided at this point to oust all its illiterate soldiers without apparently giving them any opportunity for retraining, and this first class soldier was obliged to leave the one career at which he excelled and which provided him with a respectable income. They could have used him when Vietnam came along a little later.

Vehicles were assigned to many members of my unit during their period of duty in Germany. These ranged from jeeps to five ton trucks (this was, after all, an engineering unit), with a rather smart khaki Chevrolet thrown in for good measure, as the staff car available to the officer commanding the 11th Engineer Group, a 'bird' colonel. The CO's driver was responsible for both this vehicle and a jeep. They couldn't have picked a better man for the job. Corporal Langer was obsessed with his vehicles, and spent every moment of his spare time cleaning and polishing them.

It was a rather curious fact that the paintwork of army vehicles at that time was ill-defined in terms of exact colour. As long as it represented something approaching khaki, the powers-that-be seemed satisfied. As a result, army vehicles offered considerable scope for the imaginative artist, of which there was no shortage among the troops. The motor pool gradually filled with a variety of vehicles whose colours ranged from a smart dark green, through a multitude of the more familiar khakis, all the way down to a colour on one vehicle that its proud owner described to me as vomit yellow (a colour not dissimilar to one used by the British Eighth Army when camouflaging its vehicles in the Libyan desert during World War II).

Langer was always intent on going one better. By mixing and experimenting with numerous paints, he'd come up with a paint colour so smart that it would not seem out of place adorning the coachwork of a Rolls Royce. A deep, lustrous, shimmering green was applied to his jeep, a colour all of us envied, but he jealously guarded the recipé, and we never found out how to mix it. He might just about have got away with this colour if he had left it at that (I suspect that the colonel secretly enjoyed this idiosyncratic gesture), but he decided to go the whole hog and transfer the paint to his own jeep, while the same time gilding the lily by embellishing the white stencilling on both vehicles to distinguish them from the more standard markings which military procedure dictated for other vehicles. This entailed some nice italic work, together with a smart font resembling

Times Roman which he devised for the front bumper stencils, and some rather attractive white detailing picked out around the spare wheel hub. The end result so moved him that he at once set off into town to find a metallurgist and plating plant. Following brief negotiations, a beautifully chromium plated pick and shovel appeared on the jeep, soon followed in rapid succession by similar chromium embellishments to wheel nuts, hinges and spare fuel canister.

The overall effect, it had to be admitted, was striking, and would no doubt have gained him a blue ribbon at any classic car contest back home, but it wasn't quite what a front line army had in mind, and to his eternal regret, this vehicle survived in its pristine state only a few weeks. Some spoilsport of an officer spotted it in the street and reported its unauthorised appearance to the unit's commanding officer, who had a quiet word with his driver to tone it down a bit. The colonel's staff car, however, remained an attractive high gloss forest green from the House and Garden range, with some suitable attention to detail on radiator and wheel caps. Langer had ambitions to add a silver-plated Rolls Royce flying lady to the bonnet, but was fortunately restrained by colleagues concerned for his future in the armed services.

Langer's own car, of which he was very proud, was a brand new model Chevrolet, painted in a bilious combination of lime green and pink. He took enormous care of this vehicle, keeping it cleaned and polished alongside his military responsibilities. He also disparaged anyone buying non-American vehicles, claiming that a US car could outrun any foreign rubbish. Bob saw the challenge, and rose to it, and the two set out to prove it one way or another.

Bob was convinced that the Porsche, stripped as it was, could take the Chevy over a one minute run from a standing start, and a suitable place was located nearby (a closed road) where this could be put to the test. There was a good turn-out from the unit and bets were taken. The troops seemed to be about evenly divided on where they would place their money, although secretly most hoped that the Chevy would take the honours. In the event, it did, through sheer horsepower (although both cars lost a lot of rubber in the process). However, the losers, among which I count myself, were convinced that this would not have been the case if the course had contained bends.

One other character with whom I became close was George, an extrovert Greek citizen who had lived for some years in the United States. George had accepted the draft in preference to returning to his native country, where he would have similarly faced conscription. Under the colonels who ruled Greece at that time, in spite of its membership of NATO, there was no reciprocal agreement between that country and the United States regarding conscription. George, even as a member of the US armed forces, would still have been judged eligible for the draft, and was in danger of arrest should he return to his home country for a visit. His desire to take advantage of the proximity of the base to his erstwhile home town and an opportunity for a cheap military flight conflicted with unwillingness to be arrested at the border and marched off to serve in the relatively impoverished army which served the country of his birth. Coupled with the fact that he would be treated as having gone AWOL from the US Army if he failed to return at the end of his period of leave, this trip was not a decision to be taken lightly. In the end, he elected to go, sweating blood throughout his visit, but the Greek authorities didn't tumble and he returned intact.

Why he should have been called upon to serve in either army was a mystery. His eyesight was pitifully weak and scarcely improved, as far as I could judge, by the heavy black horn-rimmed glasses he chose to wear. I couldn't conceive of his passing an eye test, but in spite of this he sported a US driving licence and owned an impressively enormous Buick sedan which he'd bought in Germany from another GI and kept on base.

George was pleased to cultivate me as a friendly native co-European and I in turn was only too happy to be the recipient of these overtures, given his possession of not just a useful but an enviable form of private transport which made the journey into Heidelberg both more comfortable and more conducive to attracting the town crumpet (which was, after all, the principal aim of any weekend pass). George could be a barrel of laughs, too, and an evening trailing around the bars of Heidelberg in his company was always a memorable way of passing the time.

There was a downside to this benefit, however. Passes expired at midnight. It was essential to be back at base camp and through the barrier before the clock struck, to avoid becoming AWOL and sentenced to such unpleasantness as extra guard duty or barracks cleaning. Heidelberg was some eight miles from Tompkins Barracks in Schwetzingen, and George reckoned he could comfortably cover this distance in eight minutes. This ignored the fact that the intervening streets were largely urban and, even in the 1950s, could be busy when the bars disgorged their customers (probably about half of whom were GIs on passes rushing to get back to base) shortly before midnight.

As the hands of the clock ticked towards the bewitching hour, I would start to make encouraging noises about packing up and leaving, George meanwhile assuring me that there was ample time. By twenty to, I was getting anxious. By a quarter to I'd be reminding George that we still had a three minute walk back to car, quite apart from having to settle the bar bill. Eventually, I would succeed in prizing him out of the bar only with around eleven minutes to go. Thus fine-tuned, and with three minutes to get to the car, the result was a hair-raising eight minute drive in which I would close my eyes and pray that neither the local nor the military police were patrolling that section of road. My terror was reinforced by George's almost total inability to make out any road signs or traffic signals once it got dark.

"Is that light red or green?" George would ask, as we hurtled towards traffic lights with the speedometer needle nudging eighty miles an hour.

By the time I had affirmed it was the former, we were already through and weaving past the fleets of Mercedes taxis carrying their sozzled fares back to camp. We generally made it, although on more than one occasion I recall watching the barrier actually descending towards the bonnet of our car as we hurtled under it and into the security of the parking area.

CHAPTER 6

In which the Limey enjoys life on the German economy

The days passed peacefully as the summer of 1957 gave way to the colder months of winter. Armies in a time of peace seem an anachronism, with time in Germany spent idly keeping equipment polished and in working order, interspersed with weekend passes into the nearest town to enjoy excellent food and even better beers.

German towns take on a charm of their own during the long winter months, with their warmly lit streets, bright shop fronts and the cosy atmosphere typically to be found in the traditional cafes and *stuben*. The Goldener Hecht, Zum Zeppls, the Kupfer Kahne, Perkeos and other popular venues for food and drink became familiar territory. Some, such as Zeppls, drew their customers from a comfortable mix of US forces and locals, while others – primarily eating places – saw few Americans, whether armed forces or tourists, and once camouflaged in 'civvies', one could feel distanced from the military.

One of our first aims after settling in was to secure a set of civilian clothes to become as invisible as possible when on pass; my first weekend pass came along well before I could consider lashing out for civvies and I still blush to remember the uncomfortable experience of sitting alone in Heidelberg's best eating places, wolfing down good food and drink under the disdainful scrutiny of local diners. A few days later I was offered (and gratefully accepted) the use of a set of clothing which a couple of months earlier I wouldn't have been seen dead in. Paper-thin, well-worn grey cotton slacks and a cheap corduroy velour jacket in a startling shade of fuchsia which would have looked fine on Little Richard, but which on me looked faintly ridiculous. The jacket was also at least two sizes too big. The effect was rounded off by a tie in fluorescent blue which the previous owner assured me was the height of fashion where he hailed from (Arkansas). Nevertheless, this was a huge improvement on military uniform, not least because I thought (over-optimistically) that this might enable me to escape the attention of any patrolling military police should I become the worse for wear while wandering the streets. I wore the ensemble for several weeks before I could afford something a little more discreet.

Of all the eating and drinking places I visited in town, my personal favourite became Schafheutle, a traditional and classic German café, sadly now long gone. It served almost exclusively the local middle-aged to elderly, who enjoyed the time honoured ritual of afternoon coffee and cakes (of a quality that would have been truly the envy of the British, still recovering from rationing and the constraints of the post-war era). The traditional *Kaffeeklatsch* – groups of older German women who would come together in the afternoons to take coffee and gossip – was still much in evidence at this time, and these were always a joy to observe discreetly from my table in the corner.

Service was a feature of these restaurants. The waitresses, in their traditional black and white uniforms, brought to mind the dying breed of 'nippies' at that time still to be found serving in the Lyons Corner Houses in London, but here, the fräuleins

Fig 11 An evening out with friends in Zeppls, November 1957.
Marvin (left), George (third from left),
"Squeaky" Putnam (third from right).

were infinitely more polite if somewhat aloof and humourless. The décor was a joy, too – strictly traditional and slightly stuffy, but undoubtedly *gemütlich*.

Shopping, as well, seemed light years in advance of what was available back in England – US Marshall Aid, followed by the period known as the *Wirtschaftswunder* (economic miracle) had boosted the German economy throughout the 1950s, and in the lead-up to my first Christmas overseas the memories of the glorious overhead illuminations along the Hauptstrasse, suspended above shops bulging with goodies of a quality not seen in Britain since before the war, remain vivid. Even the streetcars, painted in cheerful blue and white, with their jangling bells heralding their arrival at each stopping point (*Plank-stadt, Eppelheim, Industriegebiet* – funny how those names still ring out after half a century) added to the atmosphere. Their eventual banishment from the Hauptstrasse after my departure from Germany was, I still feel, a regrettable and retrograde step.

It would be wrong to give the impression that everything was available in abundance at the time, however. Coffee was strictly rationed and extremely expensive, as were cigarettes. GIs, on the other hand, were issued with ration cards to obtain these items in the PX (military shop on base), a facility which I, as a non-smoker and limited coffee drinker, derived little direct, but substantial indirect, benefit. Both could be readily traded with locals for a variety of goods and services, some of which are better left to the imagination. I also remember local friends asking me to obtain long-playing records for them, these being limited and costly on the German economy.

In my experience, there appeared to be little open antago-nism between the local German population and the Americans stationed in the area (although this may have resulted from the generally better behaviour of well-educated forces stationed at and around the US Army's European headquarters because I heard rather different stories from areas like those around Kaiserslauten where the US paras were based). Most American troops, whether officers or other ranks, showed little interest in cultivating friendships with the German population, however, and the language proved a barrier. At that time it would be rare to come across a shopkeeper or even a waiter who had more than a cursory knowledge of English. Relationships by and large were restricted to the cross-gender variety (this was long after the anti-fraternisation rules were lifted by the allied forces in Germany, and in any case these had been observed more in the breach). Many German girls were keen to get away from the perceived limitations of life in their country and were attracted by the idea of married life in America – then seen as an impossibly wealthy country. Marriages between GIs and Germans, in consequence, were by no means uncommon.

Undoubtedly, among the population as a whole, friction existed below the surface, and there were frequent incidences when tension rose within the population as a result of local girls dating GIs (*amiliebchen* – lovers of Americans – was the disparaging term used by locals to describe these relationships). A handful of places set out to cater almost entirely to the US forces stationed in the area. The most notorious of these was Rodensteiners, a huge, hideously unattractive bar just off the Hauptstrasse serving GIs whose principal ambition in life appeared to be to drink as much German lager as they could down in an evening, and to lay as many of the local girls as possible. As these two aims tend to correlate negatively, the attendant girls, generally local prostitutes, spent much of their time extracting as much money as they could from their eager punters before the latter fell asleep. Many of these young GIs, from humble Bible Belt regions of the USA, had had little or no sexual experience before their first trip overseas. Consequently they thought they'd found paradise and with money burning a hole in their pockets were anxious to maximise their new found opportunities (*pace* the messages of the training films). They learned quickly, tending to be broke for the following three weeks, and hence confined to barracks.

One amusing episode occurred early on in my new life at Schwetzingen. My Harvard-educated legal friend discovered that the American Bar Association meeting that year was to be held in London. He was determined to be present. The ABA was (and still is) one of the largest conferences in the world, then drawing at least 25,000 delegates. Many ABA members were serving with the American forces in Europe at that time, and made the decision to attend. However, these were inevitably all officers, preferring to serve their obligatory draft over three years with a commission, rather than suffering the ignominy of two years in the ranks. My friend therefore, rather mischievously, determined to attend in his PFC's uniform, and applied for leave. He thoroughly enjoyed himself, the centre of attention as officers in smart dress uniforms gazed open-mouthed at this upstart from the ranks as he worked his way through the throngs.

The humdrum life of a mail clerk offered few opportunities for excitement, with only occasional experiences to relieve the routine. On arrival at the Heidelberg central sorting office, the mail clerks met together regularly, becoming a small band of brothers and exchanging news about one another's lives in their various barracks. One with whom I became close was 'Squeaky' Putnam, a diminutive young ingénue with a high pitched voice who reminds me now of the character Radar, from the TV series M*A*S*H. He was greatly liked within his outfit, and was always well equipped with stories and scandal from the various bases around Heidelberg.

It was 'Squeaky' Putnam who passed on news from one of the mail clerks who enjoyed a rather more stimulating time than the rest of us, being attached to the Third Armoured Division, the unit to which Elvis Presley had been transferred, following his induction on March 24th 1958.

While most of us travelled backwards and forwards with small mail sacks half full of letters, this lad had a two and a half ton truck to transport Elvis's mail, and a team of helpers to sort it on arrival.

I was always sorry not to have had an opportunity to meet Elvis personally, but relished the stories about his time in uniform with which we were regaled by his mail clerk. Many of these details have been recounted in countless biographies, but we enjoyed the small titbits which were too insignificant to find a ready public, including the fact that Elvis, among his many amours while overseas, was dating the colonel's daughter, to her father's great displeasure and to the envy of his fellow GIs (she was evidently the best-looking girl around). Actually, we all had a lot of respect for Elvis, who could easily have avoided the draft by choosing to sign up for forces entertainment, but he instead determined to see his draft obligation through like any other soldier. He certainly paid the penalty in his early days under bullying NCOs who set out to take him down a peg or two.

We all enjoyed a moment of excitement when one of our fellow mail clerks was arrested for passing confidential material to the Soviets. We never quite got to the bottom of this story but evidently the lad, not the brightest apple in the orchard, had been approached in a bar by an agent and formed a friendship which culminated in passing over some low level classified material for an equally low level of remuneration.

The lad was not incarcerated, but questioned at length by military intelligence who, he told us, were, "Polite and friendly. They told me it was a trivial matter, and that if I told them everything, they were sure I wouldn't be severely penalised."

I understand a week later he was sent down for ten years in Fort Leavenworth penitentiary. Poor lad, he was really pretty harmless, if dim.

Although there had been quite a lot of emphasis on the dangers posed by the Soviet threat, the Soviet Army maintained liaison officers in the west and their vehicles were fairly common sights in and around Heidelberg. They were restricted in their travels to certain clearly defined routes and we were instructed to report their exact location to S2 – Military Intelligence – whenever we spotted one of their jeeps. I remember doing so on one occasion, having followed a Russian jeep for some three miles, but the voice on the other end of the phone appeared completely disinterested so I wondered whether to bother on a future occasion. Thinking back, I wonder whether any purpose was served by this exercise, or was it all conducted to make the ranks feel they were doing something useful to keep the peace?

Another rather gormless mail clerk in my acquaintance (what is it about mail clerks – and what does this say about me?) decided it would be fun to fly a large flag bearing the swastika from the rear of his jeep for his runs into Heidelberg – this in a country where Nazi emblems were now strictly forbidden. His was authentic. I don't know where he'd obtained it; most Germans were only too eager to burn these possessions as soon as the Allies overran their towns (although the more enterprising saw a profit opportunity, in selling them to GIs). Fortunately, the US military saw him before the German police did, and took him inside, where a short, sharp shock treatment ensured he never repeated the experiment.

Back in the mailroom, meanwhile, I and all my fellow mail clerks received new instructions: we were to stamp all outgoing letters with the words, *The US Army: A Key to Peace*. Whatever brain-dead official thought this would be a good initiative clearly wasn't reckoning on the reaction from the infuriated GIs. Several refused point-blank to allow me to stamp their homebound mail, while I in turn had to explain that mail not so franked would be withdrawn by the mail office and returned for re-franking. In protest, some went so far as to send their letters via the German postal services in preference to using the free US mail service. It made me feel there was some hope for the country. After a time, the initiative was quietly dropped.

Around this time I took the opportunity to make my first visit back home to Britain for my leave. It was a strange experience.

For some reason we were obliged to travel in military uniform, and I arrived in London smartly turned out in dress uniform but feeling neither quite British nor American. In London I transferred to the train from Victoria Station to Streatham Hill, a fifteen minute journey. I was alone in the carriage with one other passenger, an elderly gentleman in a business suit.

He eyed me in silence for a few minutes, then asked, "And where are you from, then, young man? And how do you like England?"

"From Streatham," I replied with my best South London accent, "and I love it."

Nonplussed, he relapsed into silence.

Soon after my returning to duty we had a bit of excitement in the replacement of our company commander, who rotated to the USA. His replacement was Captain Price.

Captain Price was a shock. We'd grown used to the disparity in the quality of officers with whom we came into contact during our periods of duty. Many were first class, and could obviously anticipate a long and successful career in the army. In the case of many others, we could only shake our heads with disbelief that they had succeeded not only in entering officer candidate schools, but actually gaining a commission. Captain Price, who hailed from Shreveport, Louisiana, clearly fell into the latter category.

He addressed the assembled HQ Company in his first morning assembly, looking as if he'd been celebrating his appointment throughout the previous night and, awaking only a few moments earlier, been in something of a rush to dress. His uniform resembled the contents of an untidy laundry bag – faded, creased, flecked with dirt. His belt sagged, and his holster bearing its standard issue Colt .45 was slung so low that it brushed his knee.

We stared at each another while he tried to gather his thoughts. Eventually he spoke, or rather bellowed in a high pitched nasal voice with a strong Louisiana twang: "First off… Ah expect the same haaa standards from maa men as Ah demonstrate."

Silence, followed by first a cackle, then an outright roar of laughter, as the men collapsed, helpless, in the ranks. The good Captain was nonplussed, but pursued his cause.

Sadly, the fine nuances of the rest of his address escaped me, as the accent was just too heavy, but I was later informed by my colleagues that it lived up to its promise throughout. Captain Price appeared to be a man unused to addressing large throngs, who found it difficult to know exactly what to say or how to express himself. Worse, he had difficulty, à la George W, in getting out many words consisting of more than one syllable. He was evidently under instruction to warn us of the dangers we faced from erratic German drivers when driving our cars in local streets. His first sentence included the word 'automobile'. This four syllable word defeated him. He spent a couple of minutes trying to get beyond 'auto', while we agonised for him. The idea of simply referring to a 'car' escaped him (or maybe it just wasn't in his American vocabulary). In the end, he managed just one brief admonishment, "Aw, shucks, just watch out for them Motherfuckin' Volkswagens!"

Somehow we came to feel a kind of affection for him.

The US forces make a big thing of 'field expediency' and with their belief in the individual coupled with a 'can do' mentality, they are led to believe in the ability of any man in the field, whether junior officer or lowly private, to take charge of an operation if higher ranking soldiers had been killed or wounded.

There is a simple belief among US officers that Germany lost the war in part because the hierarchical structure of their armed forces precluded discussion about tactics between the ranks and that when their officers had been eliminated, German field troops were simply incapable of continuing to fight – a legend which I believe has very limited credibility. By contrast, everyone in the American Army, be he ever so humble, sincerely believes he is capable of winning the war on his own, if only the others would listen to him.

On several occasions in the field I can remember young PFCs suggesting to the NCO in charge, "Sergeant, wouldn't it be better if we approached this in another way?"

Sergeants in turn would tolerate these interruptions to their instructions, sometimes give serious thought to the proposal (I have to admit that it would often appear to me that the new strategy might have worked more effectively), and on rare occasions would implement it. With my background in the CCF and knowledge of the much more hierarchical system which operates in the British forces, I found this tendency towards democracy rather worrying initially, but after the experience of being commanded by Captain Price, I felt positively reassured by the practice.

I did at least manage to avoid a run-in with Captain Price, whereas I had got myself into a situation with my previous CO which, to my mind, was insoluble. It was common practice among commanding officers to ask their mail clerks to undertake some dogsbody duties on their runs between the barracks and the central postal clearing point. This could entail anything from dropping off some dry cleaning to picking up a six pack of local lager. The group commander, at the time a Lieutenant-Colonel, had got to hear of these practices and determined to put a stop to them. An order had been disseminated for officers to desist from the practice, and around this time, the colonel spotted my jeep parked near a shop in Schwetzingen. He stopped me, and asked what I was doing. I had to acknowledge that I was collecting something for the company CO.

"Don't ever do that again," he warned me.

The following day, my CO asked me again to pick something up when in town. Quandary: do I listen to him, the man who directs my daily life and in whose hands any hopes of promotion lie? Or to the group CO, who outranks him, but whom I might never see again, and who scarcely knows I exist?

After wrestling with this problem for a few seconds, I decided to opt for orders from the higher authority, and expressed my regret that I had had direct orders no longer to take on such non-military tasks. Big mistake. The captain looked at me for a moment and then dismissed me without a word. However, I'm convinced that this action delayed my promotion to PFC by at least six months.

This business of following authority is a tricky one. Of course, we could always be expected to be pulled up for being 'out of uniform', if any parts of said uniform failed to conform to the code, or we were discovered not wearing a hat, for example. In fact, we were all pretty good about this and many troopers who disparaged the army in other respects took a pride in 'looking sharp' in their uniforms. Some went beyond the call of duty, seeking to outshine their buddies by adding strictly non-author-ised creases to shirts and trousers. The models here were the military police, whose carefully pressed shirts with triple vertical crease, immaculate white lanyard and gloves served as the ideal for us all.

I can recall only one clear rebellion against the authorised uniform, coming, of all sources, from the RC chaplain. Under-taking his obligatory period of national service (chaplains are commissioned as second lieutenants when serving their country) and clearly resenting the imposition of any authority apart from those emanating from his own church, our chaplain was a rebel after our own hearts, admired and loved by all, regardless of denomination. His small tilt against the windmills of authority rested on a determination to wear brown, rather than regulation black, shoes. The CO would have the occasional quiet word with him about this, but the Chaplain was adamant that while conforming in other directions, he wasn't about to give up his rights to wear the shoe colour of his choice. Rather than risk confrontation, the powers-that-be let him get away with it, merely requiring him to keep well out of the way when any Inspections General (IG) took place.

CHAPTER 7

*In which the Limey becomes an old hand,
and nearly goes to war*

Inspections General, or IGs, are an interesting experience. For anyone who has not had to face this exercise of discipline it is hard to describe the sheer amount of effort and stress that goes into preparing for the visiting general officer. I imagine the stress is felt as keenly by commanding officers, whose career progression depends upon it, as by the harassed troops who spend countless hours cleaning and polishing to present their barracks and kit in the same pristine condition as was expected of them during their basic training. Anyone who has enjoyed films of the *Carry On, Matron* genre, or who can recall the tradition of 'Matron's rounds' in hospital will have some understanding of the work entailed. My closest parallel experience in civilian life was the Research Assessment Exercises (RAEs) held in British universities which would determine their institution's income for the years that followed, and would occupy much of the staff's time over the preceding six months.

Those to whom vehicles had been delegated were also responsible for these being rigorously inspected at IGs, but in fact vehicles were also routinely inspected throughout their life to ensure they were capable of going into action at a moment's notice. The message that many of the vehicles were now getting rather long in the tooth and were hardly ideal for potential future warfare against a strongly equipped Soviet force, was apparently lost on the Department of Defense. This programme of inspection could entail any of the troops being pulled over by a team of inspectors while engaged in everyday driving duties. A vehicle would then be subject to a meticulous scrutiny of engine and bodywork, often involving someone actually crawling under the vehicle to inspect brakes, oil sump and sundry other mysteries, all of which were expected to be as clean as the upper bodywork. Even signs of slight rust on a nut, or dirty cables, would draw criticism. These and any other minor deficiencies ('gigs') such as poor paintwork, low rubber on tyres or unclean engine parts would be the subject of a report to one's CO. More serious deficiencies could result in the vehicle being impounded until these faults had been corrected. However, there was a plus side to the exercise, in that anyone obtaining a one hundred per cent clear inspection (no gigs) would be awarded a three day pass. It was fortunate for me that my vehicle was stopped in the street and checked not long before an inspection was due, and I had been putting enormous amounts of time and effort into cleaning and preparing for it. The result got me a three day pass spent in the German Alps, a pat on the back from the Colonel and a (reluctant) letter of commendation from my CO, written, I imagined, with clenched teeth.

Apart from IGs, very little interfered with the routine of the daily round. We occasionally had the opportunity to exercise our skills on the shooting range, and extended our repertoire by shooting bazookas at mock-ups of tanks. This was actually a lot of fun, although managing to acquire any accuracy with these weapons proved to be a skill beyond most of us. However, the

FIG 12 In the motor pool.
My jeep seems to be getting approval from the visiting major-general.

experience on the range was unsettling. After firing, the shells and their casings would end up a few hundred yards away in a field, alongside of which was a small ditch which we found to be occupied by locals, mainly middle-aged women. After we had fired off a few shots, these locals would sprint from their cover across the field to collect the copper casings, which had some residual value as scrap metal. We found it extraordinary that people were prepared to risk their lives to make a little extra money in this manner. We had no way of knowing when these rushes would occur, and the women had no way of knowing when there would be a lull in the firing long enough for them to collect their precious residue. Thus the bravest would take the highest risks and be first out of the ditches, while we, under instruction to open fire, would have to hope that this didn't happen to coincide with the next gallop across the field. Apparently nobody actually got killed, at least during my times on the range, but there were some frightening near misses.

My skills on the range with M1, carbine and sub-machine gun were noted, and I was duly selected to appear in the first round of a competition to put together a team for the US Seventh Army. Unfortunately for me, the weapon I was expected to use was the SMG, which, although I had managed somehow to obtain expert certification on the range during basic training, I have always found an infernal weapon to fire. It had a tendency to pull up and to the right, so that one has to have some kind of in-built mental process of adjustment to allow for this, based on no mathematical principles that I am aware of. Shooting on fully automatic, unless you get your finger off the trigger pretty quickly, you end up firing rounds into the sky or worse, the observers. My performance was mediocre at best and I didn't make it to the next round, but at least it got me a trip away from the barracks for a day or so.

Once or twice a year we were required to go out on manoeuvres, entailing a long drive to the forested regions along the West German/Czechoslovakian border. I suppose the idea of 'being close to the enemy' was designed to have some psychological effect on us, and to motivate us to take the whole thing seriously. Grafenwöhr was a favourite spot for these activities, which invariably took place at a time when the ground would be at its wettest, after the spring rains, so that we would spend most of our time engaged in removing mud from ourselves and our vehicles. Tents were pitched in a deluge of rain, during which time we all got soaked to the skin and started head colds which we were convinced would lead to pneumonia before the exercises ended. My jeep was relatively easy to handle in these conditions, but not so the heaviest five ton trucks (known familiarly to their drivers as 'mud-mashers') which tended to bog down in the sodden ground, and required a lot of man-handling to get them back into service.

One little diversion at this time was provided when panic broke out among one group in the unit who had assembled their tent and were briefly relaxing in its shade. A hornet had joined them and was frantically buzzing around inside the tent trying to find a way out... so, in rapid succession, did the lads in the tent, shrieking in terror as they dived for the exit. I being one of the inmates lost no time in joining them, but it did cause me to wonder how well we would stand up to the real threat of enemy fire, if a flying insect could create as much panic as this. Admittedly, though, it was *big*.... and it did make a lot of noise.

We envied the cavalry outfits which we came across on these occasions. The tank drivers took pleasure in chewing up as much valuable agricultural landscape as they could manage in their brief forays. Most of these lads looked as if they were still in their teens, and the appeal of a life in the army became clearer when we saw the huge enjoyment they obtained from thrashing these heavy vehicles across the country. Nobody thought very much in those days about burning fuel at four gallons to the mile, or indeed about the economics of engaging an army division in a field exercise for a couple of weeks, the cost of which must have been staggering.

Strenuous efforts were made at intervals throughout our periods of service to consider re-enlisting, or 're-upping' as common parlance had it. These efforts were largely wasted on the draftees, most of whom could anticipate returning to comfortable well-paid jobs in civilian life. Not that the sales skills of the enlistment officers were finely tuned to the market; emphasis was placed on the security which we could anticipate from a life in the army.

"It's a hard life on the outside, lads, you're much safer in here."

I could well understand that many NCOS and officers would have become institutionalised after a lifetime of service, and simply couldn't imagine what life 'on the outside' would have been like. However, this was at a time of virtually full employment back in the USA, with employers falling over themselves in the big cities to recruit staff, and few chose to consider this less than tempting offer to sign up for another three (and in some cases six) years of service. We also found it difficult to envisage a life in the army as in any way secure given that wars, or at least major skirmishes, had a tendency to break out somewhere in the world at regular intervals throughout the twentieth century, and the Americans always seemed to want to play a part in them.

I can recall only one of the enlisted men in our outfit who took the plunge, a young Hawaiian. When he was asked why (he had never appeared to be overtly enamoured with army life, although we had our suspicions as he took enormous pride in his military appearance at all times), he couldn't give any explanation apart from, "It seemed a good idea at the time." (I think they'd bought him a couple of drinks.)

By contrast, some of the NCOs who were approaching retirement after their thirty years of service were genuinely concerned about how they would manage to re-integrate into society after the security of their institutionalised world.

At this stage in the century, a life in the army might have even been attractive to some of us, given that none of us had experienced anything like direct action, or the threat of it. This was to change in the spring of 1958 when it started to look likely that the period of tranquillity was about to end. An eruption of anti-Western feeling emerged in the Lebanon, and the US declared that it would use force if necessary to protect its citizens in that country. In July US troops were sent in, following a request for assistance by President Camille Chamoun.

Our group was placed on alert and, one by one, the companies it comprised were given orders to ship out. As HQ Company, we were the last to leave. We'd packed our bags and said our goodbyes when suddenly the order was given to halt all further movements of troops. It was with an enormous sense of relief that we unpacked and returned to normal life – a relief compounded when we discovered that many of those who shipped out had their periods of service indefinitely extended. Some of the draftees were to spend up to eighteen months sitting around in tents in the Lebanese desert waiting for something to happen, in fairly grim conditions and temperatures which at times exceeded 40 degrees, until the crisis was officially decreed over. As a result, the poor devils ended up serving anything up to a year longer than their obligatory twenty-four months.

Around this time I was given an unusual request. Mail clerks can carry all kinds of material, often documents expressly marked as confidential or secret. On some occasions, we could sign for and draw a side-arm and eight rounds of ammunition to defend any attempt to relieve us of these documents, and this ruling applied particularly if required to transport top secret material. I was called in to the group commander's office one day and asked to deliver a manila envelope marked TOP SECRET to a certain senior officer in S2 (Intelligence) Division, US Army Headquarters, Heidelberg.

Wow! An opportunity to play cowboy! I hastened down to ordnance and drew my weapon, a Colt .45, practiced (inexpertly) some sharp fast draws, locked and loaded a couple of rounds and, replacing the weapon in its holster and hoping some nefarious but preferably weedy foreign agent would attempt a snatch and grab, set off for Heidelberg. It took me a few minutes, once inside the compound, to find the offices I was looking for, which proved to be a long Nissen hut with a prominent sign on the door, *Do not proceed beyond these doors without authorised clearance.* Smaller letters indicated that I stood the risk of being shot if I chose to disobey these instructions.

Now, I was in a quandary. I had received clear orders to deliver the package personally to the individual at this address, but I had no written authority to enter the building. Weighing up the pros and cons, and deciding that execution would only follow in extreme cases and at very last resort, I plucked up courage, pushed the door open and entered. I was faced with a long, deserted corridor lined with doors, each of which bore the name and title of a senior officer of the rank of colonel or above. About half way along the corridor I located my quarry, knocked and was invited to enter.

I found the officer seated behind an enormous desk. The entire room appeared to be covered in documents. They were piled on top of his desk, on the floor next to it, and filled every available crevice of the shelves and filing cabinets surrounding him.

Saluting sharply, I identified myself and my mission, and surrendered the documents. He looked unsurprised to see me and invited me to take a seat while he busied himself in the adjacent office to provide me with the required receipt. He was absent for just a couple of minutes, but in that time I lay back in my chair and idly glanced around the room. My gaze fastened on the wall behind me, and I was instantly transfixed…

A huge map occupied the entire space of the wall. On it was drawn what appeared, to my untutored eye, to be the entire invasion plans for an attack on the Soviet Union.

Zoweeee!!

For a few seconds, I couldn't tear myself away from this spectacle. Long arrows in purple and red swept across the map from West to East, points of penetration clearly encircled. Too much information.

I hastily returned my gaze front and centre. After a moment my officer returned, handed me my receipt and invited me to disappear, which I did with alacrity. I've often thought since about that experience. Was this in fact an actual provisional plan, or a theoretical exercise? And how many others like me would have had the opportunity to wander into this innermost sanctum and cast their eyes over such a spectacle? What would they have made of it? Did this reveal a flagrant disregard for security, or was my record considered so above reproach that I could be trusted with the observation of such confidential material? But I wasn't even an American citizen! My mind went back to the experience of my Sudeten friend Hans, during basic training, when most rigorous checks had been undertaken simply to ensure he could be inducted as a lowly private!

Moments like this helped to relieve the boredom of routine duties and, indeed, this might have been the high point of my adventures in the American Army were it not for a chance event which was to change my life – not just in the service but for the rest of my days.

CHAPTER 8

In which the Limey meets someone special

Earlier I described how it was my intention, as soon as possible after I had settled in, to start German lessons so as to obtain some long-term benefit from my life in the country. Enquiries about suitable courses at the Goethe Haus and other venues in town had drawn a blank and I'd rather let the idea lapse. However, towards the end of 1957 my friend George, who had started seeing a German girl studying at Heidelberg University, approached me in pimp mode.

"Barbara has a girlfriend who'd be just great for you," he said. "Plenty upstairs..." (I took it as read that his reference was not to her intellect, but somewhere further south.) "She'd be great to learn German with."

By coincidence I was with George a few days later on pass in Heidelberg when his friend Barbara appeared in sight accompanied by my prospective German tutor. Introductions followed and we all headed off to enjoy a beer together.

Immy (her real name was Irmgard but none of my GI friends were capable of handling this and after experiencing a variety of attempts, culminating in Wormgard, we got frightened and decided to opt for something simpler) was an intriguing and enthusiastic student of languages at the university who jumped at the chance of teaching me German as a means of eking out her pocket money while a student. I made a date and we met up to talk about everything under the sun except, as it turned out, the subject of German lessons (her English was, it goes without saying, more than competent). This culminated in an animated discussion on the topic of whether ants had souls. Plans for formal lessons in German faded into the background. We found too many other things to talk about and soon moved on from a tutor/student relationship to something more intimate.

By the summer of 1958, this had reached a point where we both recognised that we were going to end up in a long term relationship, and we set about looking into the necessary documentation required for a military marriage. This involved two approaches, to the German authorities and to the US military. The former required the usual bureaucratic documentation along with appropriate translations into the English language, with which I had great fun – particularly getting my tongue round the essential *Polizeilichesfuehrungszeugnis* (the certificate issued by the German authorities indicating a clean police record).

The US military, however, largely depended upon an interview with the proposed spouse, which was one of the more hysterical experiences of my army life. My impending wife was called in for interview with the master sergeant, while I waited outside the room. The interview was carried out with both of them standing in the middle of a busy office while the sergeant tried to make himself heard above the buzz of conversation of numerous clerks. He seemed surprised that Immy had any knowledge of the English language (how do other GIs with girlfriends get to this point? I wondered) and his line of questioning, brief as it was, centred largely on whether she had ever been, or was now, a member of, or sympathised with, the Communist Party. No questions about her or her family's possible affiliation with the Nazi Party during the previous war (right wing extremism was clearly not perceived as a threat to the American way of life).

This reminded me of the extraordinary interview in which I had had to participate when seeking my US immigrant visa two years earlier. Called to the US embassy in London, I was to be faced with a string of questions about my political leanings and possible moral laxity. Just before being called in for my own interview, I witnessed a stout and immaculately turned-out businessman (complete with bowler hat and brolly) emerge from the previous interview. Purple with fury, he strode through the waiting room towards the exit shouting at no one in particular, "My God, do I *look* like the kind of man who has been living on immoral earnings?"

Anyway, my proposed spouse appeared to pass the test with flying colours and we were granted the necessary documentation to allow the marriage to proceed. We were married in a civil ceremony by the registrar in Heidelberg in September, 1958, witnessed only by two student friends from the university. Since the ceremony was conducted in German and the registrar had no English, a young female interpreter was provided. The registrar launched into a long, impassioned speech about the union of two cultures, something about the flowering of a new Europe and similar hyperbole, most of which we failed fully to take in. This was delivered with enormous sincerity, while the interpreter dissolved into floods of emotional tears. The four of us did our best to control our laughter. A few giggles at the outset gave way to near collapse, our friends on each side soon reduced to helpless laughter, while we did our best, none too successfully, to look as though we were treating the whole occasion with appropriate decorum.

A month later, a religious ceremony sealed the marriage at

a church near Immy's home village close to the Dutch border, and we took off for our honeymoon. This was planned rather haphazardly, with the idea that we would travel by train to Paris, spend a couple of nights there before moving on to Geneva and end up on the French Riviera. We caught the overnight train from Düsseldorf to Paris, having booked a four berth economy sleeper for the trip (the best I could do on a PFC's salary).

Things started to go wrong almost immediately. As we made our way along the train's corridor, we were overtaken by a stout man in a hurry, who trod heavily on Immy's foot as he passed. She shrieked in pain, to which he made no acknowledgement and rushed on. Cursing him, we hobbled to our couchettes and turned in for the night. Immy opted for a lower bunk and I took the other lower. The upper berths were already occupied and an unkempt individual above her was seated on the edge of his bunk and in the process of removing his malodorous socks, now three inches from her nose.

Immy looked despondent. "This is not the first night of marriage I was anticipating," she wailed.

Her mood didn't improve when we got to Paris, where I rashly decided it would be a good idea to look up a former girlfriend. Bad move – although she made us both very welcome.

Moving on to Geneva, we found a pleasant small hotel in a back street, where we were awakened in the early hours of the morning by a raid from the morality police demanding to see our passports to ensure we were married (the Swiss were ultra-prim in those days). Our next stop was Juan-les-Pins, where our first night there was interrupted in what seemed to us to be the early hours of the morning with a waiter delivering breakfast in bed and the morose news, *Le pape est mort*.

On a side trip to Monte Carlo for the day, we enjoyed a meal in a restaurant along the waterfront where I chose fish and managed to get a bone stuck in my throat. This necessitated a trip to a doctor, but Monaco is the kind of place where GPs don't operate – everyone is a specialist. We ended up visiting an Ear, Nose and Throat specialist who deftly removed the fishbone, then invited us into his office to determine the bill.

He looked at me, and my rather sorry looking clothes, for a moment, and asked what I did for a living.

"I'm in the army," I told him.

"Ah, I see," he replied, and sighed. He wrote out a bill far smaller than I had expected, and I silently thanked his benevolence and understanding.

Our final port of call was Nice. Now, Nice in high season was an expensive place to stay even then and accommodation was limited. However, five years earlier, in company with a friend from work, I had hitch-hiked to the South of France with the intention of spending a night in the town when we arrived. Looking for somewhere cheap, we had located what appeared to be a small *pension* on a street close to the seafront. We enquired from the elderly and inquisitive madame at the desk whether she had a vacant room for the night. She looked at us for a moment before replying, as if sizing us up, then offered us a twin bed room at what seemed a remarkably reasonable price, which we were only too happy to accept.

She showed us up to the room, which was decorated in a garish red and gold wallpaper with long velour drapes across the windows and above the beds. This seemed a bit over the top for such a modest establishment but given the price we didn't feel justified in querying the décor, so settled in happily enough, and she withdrew. After her departure, however, we walked out onto the small balcony and quickly realised we had hit on the red light district. There followed an educational evening watching the girls operating on the street below.

In the morning the old crone asked us how we had enjoyed our stay. We were effusive in our praise and I spent a half hour or so in animated discussion (my French was more than up to this, having spent a year at school in Switzerland) with the good soul, who wanted to know everything about us and what had brought us to the south of France.

Bidding us farewell, she called out, "I hope you will stay with us again if you come back to Nice, Mr Holloway." I promised I would.

So, here I was in Nice again, and my first thought was that this would be the ideal accommodation at which to stay and thus save on expense – but I was (fortunately, as it turned out) careful to have explained to Immy en route how I had come to know of the place, and the nature of its trade. We made our way to the street, and I was delighted to find that the *pension* was still where it had been five years earlier.

We walked into the lobby and I immediately recognised the madame as the good lady who had looked after us on my previous visit. She looked up at us, and didn't miss a beat. "Ah, Monsieur Holloway... how nice to see you back here again!"

In spite of my having mentioned my earlier visit to Immy, I got a funny look from her at this point.

On our return to duty in Germany, I applied to move 'onto the economy'. This was a relatively straightforward procedure for married soldiers stationed abroad, subject to just one criterion: we had to live close to the barracks and to be reachable quickly in the event of a crisis. This meant in practice having a phone, or access to a phone. Getting phones installed in Germany in the late 1950s was no easy matter, and delays of several weeks, if not months, could be anticipated.

A small settlement, Hirschacker, had sprung up in the immediate vicinity of the camp, largely to meet the needs of the US forces for accommodation (today, this has grown to become a sizeable suburb of Schwetzingen) and a number of locals had seized the opportunity to cash in by building buy-to-let properties in the area. No thought was given to the design of these hideous erections, which took the form of square blocks constructed of unpainted breezeblock cemented together with an equally unattractive grey mortar. However this was better than living on base and remaining separated, so after a bit of research we discovered one GI from our company who lived in the village and possessed a telephone. Evidently every other soldier from the unit living off-base had likewise discovered this poor chap and had given the authorities his phone number as contact when alerts were called. The result of this was foreseeable...

When our first practice alert was called, the GI with the telephone had to rush around the village knocking on twenty or so doors to raise us. Given that we were supposed to be ready to move out in about twenty minutes, and that most of the fellow GIs were sleeping off a heavy night in the bar, this proved an impossible task, and the military imposed a limit on the number of 'contacts' that would be permissible in future. Fortunately I was by then getting close to the end of my period of service overseas, and this restriction didn't affect me.

Hirschacker wasn't just depressing for its residential buildings. The sole public building in the village was a bar patronised exclusively by GIs, their wives, mistresses and miscellaneous girlfriends. The interior contained the most seedy and gloomy pub décor that I've ever come across, before or since. It was a place for serious drinking and little attempt had been made to relieve the gloom engendered by this purpose. The lighting, if I remember accurately, consisted of naked neon bulbs which were generally obscured by a pall of cigarette smoke hanging over the room. The latter actually helped to disguise the poverty of the décor to some extent.

The corridor leading to the bar area was dingy and narrow, and more often than not littered with the recumbent forms of soldiers sleeping off the effects of too much lager (the US troops never did come to terms with the strength of the German beers). These, one was obliged to step over. If anything, this place was even more depressing than the awful enlisted men's bar on base – and the beer was pricier, although infinitely better. However after one or two visits I decided it would be worth the extra effort of a trip to Schwetzingen, or even Heidelberg, rather than the dubious entertainment to be found in this location.

The couple who rented us a room in their house were typical of the householders struggling to make a living in the area. The room we had taken on was tiny, and fitted with a single 2'6" bed, onto which we valiantly clung and from which I, heroically having taken up the outside position, would fall with monotonous regularity onto the hard linoleum floor.

Frau Bermann was a pleasant little woman, rather dominated by her burly and macho husband, a builder. He, meanwhile, tended to see me as a challenge, so different from his own culture and a reluctant drinker at the best of times. He threw occasional taunts in my direction, most of which were lost on me with my limited understanding of the language, but I did get eventually that he wanted to share a drink with me and wasn't about to take no for an answer. His objective was transparent; to drink me under the table. At that time, I enjoyed the odd beer, but felt that three pints in an evening was as much as I was comfortable with. In my teens I had on occasion drunk eight or nine pints without any noticeable difference in behaviour beyond a tendency to fall asleep eventually, so I reluctantly agreed to his invitation and we sat down to enjoy 'a pint or two' in his sitting room.

What I hadn't counted on was Herr Bermann ringing the changes, by interspersing the lagers with shorts of Schnapps. His idea was clearly to render me incapable as quickly as possible. We sank a beer, followed by a schnapps, followed by a beer, followed by a schnapps... I don't know exactly how long we both kept this up, but I was determined not to be beaten and remained as impassive as ever. Bermann meanwhile grew more jovial by the minute, then aggressive and finally sullen until – suddenly, placing his half finished beer glass on the table – he gently slid from his seat onto the floor where he promptly fell sleep.

In the morning, none the worse for wear, he greeted me with new-found respect and we enjoyed a healthy, if distant, relationship for our remaining weeks in Hirschacker.

CHAPTER 9

In which life in the army comes to an end,
after the Limey experiences a little local difficulty

My period of service overseas was coming to an end. My normal date of rotation would have been in January the following year, but regulations allowed for earlier rotations from overseas, and I was offered the opportunity to leave in December of that year by ship from Bremerhaven.

Shortly before this, however, we received a final IG inspection at Tompkins Barracks, which of course would routinely include a thorough inspection of my mailroom. The general officer duly called at my room and went through my documentation with care. It was up to date and immaculate, and he congratulated me.

He then paused for a moment, having heard my replies to his question, and dropped the bombshell I had feared. "You are, I take it, an American citizen?"

"Er, well, actually, no, Sir," I faltered.

The shit hit the fan. After the expected remonstrations, the powers that be had to decide what action at this stage was necessary. It was determined that an immediate top security clearance would have to be undertaken on my background, to be completed before I left military service. Evidently, this would keep the paperwork in order. Hence, a clearance that would normally have taken at least three months would need to be undertaken within three weeks.

They managed it – just. And this involved examinations into my life in the UK before coming to the States, as well as interviews with my colleagues at work in New York. Strangely, they didn't impose any sanctions on me at all, not even asking me directly whether I had been aware of the citizenship ruling – which I would have had to have been, if I were familiar with the mail clerk's duties. I suppose, given the short duration of my remaining time in the service, they thought it simply not worth bothering about.

My final days in Germany were spent walking around with the same seraphic smile on my face as I had observed on others during their final weeks of service, "Man!! Am I short!"

In early December I entrained with a handful of other blissfully happy enlisted men from my barracks and, after tearful farewells to wives and girlfriends (and in some cases, both), we headed for the North Coast. We happy band of innocents didn't know that the good old boys in the military had one final trick up their sleeves for us: the North Atlantic in mid-winter.

The flight over to Europe eighteen months previously had been bad news, but what we faced now, unbeknown to us, was to be infinitely worse. We gazed with dismay at the rust bucket that was to be our home for the next 14 days. USS *Geiger* was well past her sell by date, and would probably have been retired had she not been fulfilling a useful role in transporting grunts across the big pond.

With some trepidation we embarked and made our way into the bowels of the ship to the sleeping area which was to become our home for the duration. It was a vast space containing three tiers of bunks with scarcely a gap between each large enough to raise one's head. A good friend had passed on valuable advice about travel by military ship; make sure you get the top bunk. This avoided the unpleasant but commonplace experience of having those above you throw up over your head when it got a bit rough. Most of the others, unaware of this morsel of information, headed for the bottom bunks to avoid the climb, so I had no difficulty staking my claim to a top bunk. These also had more headroom, and avoided the inevitable bumps on the head that resulted when first awakening and sitting up with a shock, wondering where the hell we were.

There were also routine duties to be performed during our crossing. We'd forgotten what it was like, in our pampered lives in German barracks, to have to pull KP or any of the other unpleasant roles expected of us. It fell to me to take on the role of night baker, working through the night and sleeping by day. A handful of us were given over to the charge of an enormous African-American NCO, the kind of character you'd expect to see in TV's Sergeant Bilko series. As master baker, he ran the show, and he believed in working us hard. It became our duty each night to knead the dough for several thousand rolls that would be consumed on board each day. We then cut and shaped the dough before assisting our despotic overlord to feed the results into the huge ovens.

The work was hard, physically exhausting and mind-blowingly repetitious, while the galleys were unbearably hot with all ovens in continuous operation. The smell of bread, something I normally enjoy, soon became overpowering and as the vessel began to run into bad weather, made us all physically sick. We were crying out for some fresh air – and we got some soon enough.

About three days into the voyage, the storm hit us. As a

previous employee of a shipping company, I was used to bad weather on the Atlantic during my regular crossings, so seasickness had never been a problem for me. But this was something else. A full force hurricane hit us and stayed through a number of days, keeping track of the vessel.

The pattern of life on board requires all troops to leave their bunks and sleeping quarters in the morning and make their way up on deck, regardless of weather, so that areas below deck can be thoroughly cleaned each day by a posse of 'volunteers'. We went below only to eat, until the evening, when we could descend to the bars and enjoy what passed for entertainment on board.

We first knew we were in for a bit of a blow when we emerged on deck on day three. With some effort, I forced open the door leading onto the deck, to find myself staring into a wall of sea with no evidence of a horizon. I was granted little time to work out how this was possible, because the next moment I found myself looking at a similar wall of sky. I realised that we were tilting well over 45 degrees on each roll of the ship. The forward motion was equally unsettling, with the bow crashing into waves which swept across the decks and soon had us soaking wet. We imagined that no one could stay out on deck in these conditions, and so awaited orders for us all to make our way below once again. Such naiveté!

An hour later, with no sign of any orders coming over the tannoy, we accepted that we were to spend the morning at least on deck. We lashed ourselves as best we could to davits, bollards, rails or anything else stationary and offered up prayers in preparation for our fate. Discomfort is one thing but with three quarters of the troops seriously seasick the decks were soon awash with vomit. Notwithstanding the stiff winds that lashed us, the stench became unbearable, making even the old sea dogs among us distinctly queazy.

The weather kept this up, with varying intensity, for the best part of six days, by which time we were exhausted and many were having difficulty keeping any food down. At least the rain had slackened off, and we even enjoyed some glorious sunshine towards the end of the voyage. Things settled down enough for me to even contemplate enjoying a few drinks below decks, and I joined in with some of the games taking place during the evenings. This included bingo, with a rolling tote which had accumulated to the sum of more than $600 by the final evening. And blow me down – I won it! I, who never won anything, and didn't even bother to gamble in the ordinary way, but was just trying to pass the time as painlessly as possible.

$600 was a sizeable amount in those days, and gave me more than a much needed head start for my return to civilian life. Nevertheless, I was never more glad to get ashore in New York from any ship in my life as, weak and wobbly, we finally made our way down the gangplank, and I realised my days of night bakery were behind me. I've never felt quite the same about the smell of baking bread since.

The same day found us back at Fort Dix for processing. This took a few days, accompanied by the usual round of meaning-less duties (mine involved emptying garbage bins in the early hours of the morning). Some items of our kit we had to turn in (I was really sorry to have to surrender my parka) but most of it stayed with us – I still have the dress uniform and a pair of well-soled army boots in the attic, although sadly neither fit me very well; the waist of my trousers in particular seems to have shrunk in the cold of the attic storage.

On the final day of processing we were obliged to attend a series of lectures designed to equip us for civilian life as good citizens. For this exercise we were honoured with an address by a general officer who spent several minutes offering dire warnings about the threats we were about to face, in particular the red menace. This fifteen minute speech was followed by a short film showing a crowd of happy New Yorkers celebrating the New Year in Times Square.

A voice-over from the General interrupted the commentary. "Now, these all seem happy citizens innocently enjoying themselves, right? OK, I want you to concentrate on the figure in the extreme top left corner of the screen. See what he's up to?"

A highlight circled the figure in question, so small as to be barely made out among the vast throng. He appeared to be holding his arm aloft, with his fist clenched.

"A Commie!" exploded the General through gritted teeth. "This is what you've got to look out for – subversives in our communities. They're everywhere. Always be on your guard."

We looked at one another with amazement. The McCarthy period was, we thought, long dead. Yet paranoia was clearly still present among the leading echelons in the military. The lights went up and we were dismissed with another reminder always to watch out for the menace of undercover Communism, from wherever it might emerge.

My final document discharging me from active service was accompanied by a report on my physical and mental state, confirming that, should I so desire – and if I acted quickly – I could re-enlist within the next ninety days as long as I didn't pick up any diseases in the interim.

I wasn't tempted.

Our military commitment wasn't quite complete with the termination of active service, however. Theoretically, we were required to undertake a further two years in the active reserve at a 'nearby' depot, before being transferred for an additional two year period to the inactive reserve, on stand-by and subject to recall to military service in the event of a national emergency.

The limitation of military resources in the New York area meant that I could not be assigned immediately, but a few months later they caught up with me and assigned me to a unit in Long Island City. This was about as inconvenient as it could have been, necessitating a trip by bus from my home on Staten Island to the ferry across the bay to Manhattan, thence a long subway journey to the unit's location in the borough of Queens. The travel time far exceeded the period of military training upon which I was supposed to be engaged for one evening a week, over the remaining two years of my obligation.

Curiously, I have virtually no memory of what I actually did throughout those long boring evenings. However, as one requirement of service on active reserve I was required to complete another period on manoeuvres and the date I was given happened to coincide with the time when my wife, who had by now joined me in New York, was due to give birth to our first child. So I applied for a postponement of this obligation, to be assigned at a later date. This was something I was very reluctant to do, because not only would I not be serving among soldiers that I had come to know well, but I soon appreciated that reservists who have failed to attend their compulsory period of field manoeuvres were for the most part skivers, and were treated as such.

The army uses the term 'obligors' to describe those either postponing their duties or deliberately trying to avoid them. We soon learned that we were a despised lot when I, accompanied by one other soldier, reported for duty. We were instructed to report to the military training centre at Camp Drum near Watertown in upstate New York. A more desolate and depressing area of the State it would be hard to find. Watertown was then (maybe it still is) an impoverished settlement depending very largely on the presence of the nearby army camp, offering little in the way of diversion apart from a few seedy bars and porno bookshops. There was, in any case, little opportunity to sample the pleasure of either of these because our brief sojourn in the area would be limited to the backwoods. After a chewing out from the NCO to whom we two 'obligors' reported, we were sent off to clean the barracks windows, as the rest of the units assigned to the field had already embussed and were somewhere out in the wilderness.

A morning spent window cleaning is, I suppose, preferable to gallivanting around the less salubrious regions of upstate New York, and we wondered whether we were condemned to pass our time in other equally pointless activities.

In the afternoon a young officer entered the barracks, and pointed to us. "You two," he bawled. "Can either of you play an instrument?"

Without a second's hesitation, we both affirmed that we could. OK, maybe we would be caught out later, but anything was better than a week of KP activity.

"OK", he grunted. "You're assigned to the PX."

We trundled off to report, and the next thing we knew, we were each assigned a small truck and a vast supply of nibbles – chocolate, candy, crackers, soft drinks – and instructed to get out in the field, find the troops and sell.

This looked like a doddle, and it was. It took a bit of time trying to track down where the units were based, but once I'd located mine, I was welcomed like a long lost friend. There were fixed periods when we were expected to throw open the back of the vehicle and dispense our wares. An abiding memory is the assortment of muddy, tired GIs who, after a morning's frantic activity, now waited patiently in line to buy their candy bars.

"Man, have you got it easy!" said the first trooper in line enviously, and I had to admit that I had.

For a week, this was the sum total of our 'field training' – at least I became adept at handling small change, even though the job didn't require much in the way of sales skills. We slept in barracks, while thinking fondly of the rest of the unit in their pup tents, and ate in comfortable mess rooms. It was almost with a sense of disappointment that I returned to civilian life and real work a week later.

My week in the field almost drew to a close my time in the army, although it was another two years before the final letter came through, which removed me from the inactive reserve to full civilian status. My discharge paper, dated 31 December 1962 offered, "Grateful appreciation of your faithful military service to the Nation" and somewhat ominously hoped I would, "Maintain my interest in the army so that you may be better oriented in the event that your services should again be required in a national emergency."

No thanks – I'm outta here.

Thinking back to those times, I thank God that Vietnam hadn't yet started, and realised how naïve I had been in accepting a commitment to two years in the army of a country I hardly knew, and which has since gone on to see active service in so many unattractive parts of the world. I might have so easily been obliged to spend my two years under fire in Afghanistan or Middle Eastern hell holes if the conflagrations which have unsettled the world in the past two decades had occurred a little earlier in history.

Today, at least, the Draft is history and the US troops now serving around the world are there as volunteers, whether as members of the regular army or the National Guard.

Would I have chosen the Draft option in today's world? No way.

Would I do the same thing all over again, given the circumstances of the day? A qualified yes. I got a lot out of the experience, not least an ideal wife, a number of lifelong friends and the pleasure of meeting a wonderful bunch of colourful characters.

I was to spend a further eight years in the States after completion of my military service before my company eventually transferred me back to our head office in the UK and my life as a trainee American ended.

Years later, back in Britain, I became a fan of M*A*S*H, recognising how close this series was to real life in the service, with all its black humour and colourful characters. The camaraderie among a tight knit military community, even in a peacetime army, is something seldom found in everyday life, and I felt enriched by this experience, as evidenced by how much of it I still remember fifty years on. The good bits remained with me for life; most of the bad bits aren't even memories.

Am I sorry not to have re-upped? You've got to be kidding!